DEVONSHIRE YEAR

An Illustrated Journal of the Jurassic Coast & Countryside

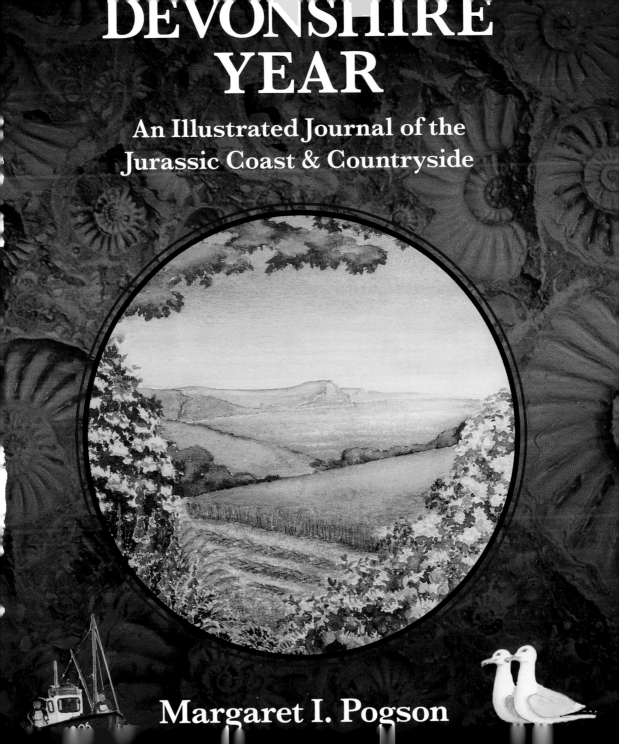

Margaret I. Pogson

Doug Brown's fishing boat *Bambi*, **Seaton Beach**

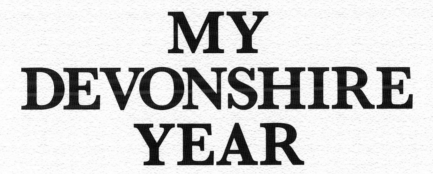

MY DEVONSHIRE YEAR

An Illustrated Journal of the Jurassic Coast & Countryside

Margaret I. Pogson

Richard Webb, Publisher, Dartmouth, Devon

DEDICATION
by Brian Pogson
For Mother, Dad and James

First published in the United Kingdom in 2015 by Richard Webb, Publisher

First impression July 2015

A CIP catalogue record for this book is available from the British Library

ISBN 978-0-9568464-4-0

Typesetting: Titling: Baskerville Bold   Body copy: Baskerville Regular

• 224 pages • 224 illustrations including 220 in colour • 32,000 words • 245mm x 175mm
Printed on 170gsm Essential Silk matt paper
with Forest Stewardship Council certification

Fossil green endpapers: Copyright © 2001-2012 Mayang Murni Adnin

***My Devonshire Year* was designed, printed, distributed and published
exclusively by these West Country companies**

Photography by Jon Robinson-Pratt ABIPP, Exmouth, Devon

Designed by Laurence Daeche, Anon Design Co., Christchurch, Dorset

Printed and bound by SRP, Exeter, Devon   www.shortrunpress.co.uk

Distributed by Tormark, Redruth, Cornwall   www.tormark.co.uk

Published by Richard Webb, Dartmouth, Devon
www.dartmouthbooks.co.uk   Email: mail@richardwebb.co.uk

CONTENTS

My Devonshire Year

INTRODUCTION BY BRIAN POGSON

Brian Pogson on the Cobb at Lyme Regis in 1987 *By kind permission of Phil Lockley*

On her 80th birthday, 6th October 2014 my Mother lovingly gave me her personal and heartfelt tribute to Devon, her beautifully illustrated and hand written journal *My Devonshire Year*.

Her book is a time capsule of Devon's Jurassic coast in 1979, over twenty years before it became a UNESCO World Heritage site in December 2001. Her handwritten accounts of the weather, flowers, wildlife and country life are accompanied by her detailed watercolour illustrations. These include flora and fauna, the coastline, seascapes and the Devon countryside and a few capture men at work. I even make an appearance hauling pots out at sea on Bimbo Turner's fishing boat *Bimbo's Boy*.

It took my Mother six years and a great deal of dedication and commitment to complete the illustrations. Her attention to detail was incredible with much time spent researching the various flora and fauna to ensure her record was accurate. She has always had a great love of flowers and kept beautiful cottage gardens. She would pick some of the plants and paint them, but the rare ones she would paint in place.

When my Mother had completed her journal she had the book bound by a company in Exeter. I remember her telling me that when she went back to collect it, the man took it out of the shop safe, it was all wrapped up in oil cloth and, as he revealed it, and she saw her finished work for the first time, all she could do was to cry.

For decades the journal was kept safely in a drawer and occasionally brought out to show visitors. I had not seen it for more than twenty years but, as I began to turn the pages, it was clear the illustrations were as bright and clear as the day my Mother had painted them. It reminded me of an earlier period of my life at home as a teenager when I recall my Mother going off to paint. My Dad would drop her off on his motorcycle in the middle of the countryside with her paints and sandwiches and she would sit there painting. Dad would return to collect her later.

My parents moved from Lincolnshire to Devon in 1970 when I was nine years old and, seeing my Mother's work again after all these years, evoked memories that made me realise the significance that this move to Devon had made on her life and the impact it had on mine.

When we relocated from Boston, Lincolnshire to a top floor flat on the seafront in Seaton, for me, it is where my life began as I was now living virtually on the beach! I used to go down to the seashore with my Mother when she was painting the fishing boats. My Mother had a folding stool she would sit on and she would put a piece of paper onto her board with masking tape to hold it in place. While my Mother was painting, I would chat to the fishermen and it wasn't long before I was going out to sea hauling lobster pots – sometimes before school. It is no wonder I later became an inshore fisherman and I loved it. I commercially fished from Lyme Regis for twenty years.

Turning the pages of my Mother's journal is like a familiar journey through my life. I have lived and worked here since I was nine years old and every page is a reminder of how beautiful Devon is and how fortunate I am that my parents made the move here. In 1987 I got married in Axmouth Church and we began married life in the village of Axmouth before moving to Rousdon. My wife and I have three sons who went to school in Uplyme and then Lyme Regis. As a family we share many fond memories of the local area - times spent in the Undercliff, on Charton beach and at local events, various fêtes, and even a spectacular firework display, one Bonfire night, at the former Allhallows School. My wife and I still live nearby, now in a village near Axminster.

I vaguely recall my Mother mentioning visits to Devon when she was a child but I had never really paid much attention to the reason we moved to Devon, other than family holidays and because my Dad had acquired a new job. Talking with my Mother, and carrying out my own research, I discovered that my grandfather's (Albert Robert Fost) parents were both born in Axminster, Devon.Furthermore, my great grandmother was formerly a Gapper whose brother Richard Gapper lived at the Landslip Cottage *(see panel below and page 146)* in the Undercliff below Dowlands, Rousdon. In her journal, my Mother recalls visiting Richard's wife, Auntie Mary and their daughter Annie at the Landslip Cottage with her father when she was a child - the fading memories of a bygone era.

My Mother's book holds a special place in my heart for its significance to me personally but it also takes the reader on a calm and peaceful journey that follows the rhythm of the seasons. It opens ones' eyes to nature and the countryside. It has been a hidden treasure that I have now chosen to share so that it can be enjoyed by others.

Brian Pogson

Above left: **The Landslip Cottage** *(see page 146)* **in the Undercliff home to Richard Gapper** *(Far right)* **brother of Elizabeth Fost née Gapper) and Mary Gapper**

Above centre: **Wedding photograph of Margaret's parents Albert Robert Fost and Irene Hunt** *(front row centre).* **Fred Fost** *(back row far left)* **and Elizabeth Fost née Gapper** *(back row second from left)*

THE AUTHOR: MARGARET I. POGSON

Passport photo of Margaret aged 19

Although Margaret's grandparents were from Devon and Dorset, she was born on 6th October 1934 in Ilkeston, Derbyshire. Its major industries used to be coal mining, iron working and lace making.

Margaret's father, Albert Robert Fost, was a Railway Signalman for LNER. She lived in Ilkeston for two years with her mother Annie Irene and her brother Bernard Jeffrey, before moving to Hadley Wood in North London where her father ran Greenwood Signal Box, New Barnet. It is on the East Coast Main Line between London Kings Cross and Edinburgh.

Margaret's father, Albert Robert Fost outside the signal box at Kirkby la Thorpe, Lincolnshire in 1951

Margaret was educated at Minchenden Grammar School, Southgate, North London. Her mother used to paint and that inspired Margaret who when only 14, won a competition in a gardening magazine for painting flowers. At the age of 15 they all moved to a gate house at Kirkby la Thorpe on the Lincolnshire Fens where her father ran the signal box.

It was here that Margaret met her future husband, Kenneth. He was a railway fireman regularly passing this signal box on the branch line and when on the express routes fired famous engines like the *Flying Scotsman*, *Britannia* and the *Mayflower*.

On Early Shift, Greenwood Signal Box, New Barnet, London 1948

Margaret and Kenneth Pogson on their Wedding Day

Margaret married Kenneth on 17th October 1955 and they moved to Boston in Lincolnshire.

They had two sons, James born on 16th May 1959 (died on 17th September 2010) and Brian born on 28th September 1961.

Margaret went to evening classes to learn to paint at Kitwood School, Boston when the boys were young, as she wanted to do a correspondence course in textile and design as they grew older.

The teacher invited her to join the local Art Society which she found very daunting as they were all professionals.

Margaret and Brian in the Lym Valley, Lyme Regis 1970

SEATON, DEVON

At the Art Society she met a very bold and burly Yorkshire man who painted in watercolour and had done a picture of a field full of cabbages which she said was beautiful.

She told him she wanted to paint like him and he advised her to only paint in watercolours and nothing else until she had mastered the art.

Her husband Ken left the railway in 1961 and became an ambulance man. The family moved to Seaton in Devon in 1970 where Ken ran the local Ambulance Station.

They lived in a top floor flat with a roof garden on the seafront with panoramic views of the surrounding countryside, marshes, beach, seascape and the Jurassic Coast.

Margaret was a founder member of the Seaton District Art Society and became its Secretary.

The Art Society used to invite a London artist called Harry Richardson down to Seaton to give a painting week each year. He taught Margaret how to paint flowers in watercolour and how to create shadows.

She decided to paint a book on the coast and countryside because her husband was considering moving the family back to Lincolnshire. Margaret wanted a record to remind her of the beauty of Devon if she had to leave.

Margaret wrote and illustrated *My Devonshire Year* in 1979 and the family stayed in Devon where she continued to paint and enjoy the natural world around her.

Margaret painting a landscape in the grounds of Bindon Manor, Axmouth while on a painting week with Seaton Art Society in the late 1970s

In 1986 they moved to a cottage in the village of Axmouth where she created a beautiful country garden inspired by her love of traditional Devon country flowers and old fashioned roses. It was Margaret's intention to paint another book documenting her country garden and life. She bought the paper but her love for her garden consumed her time and the second book was never started.

She was delighted to give Brian, her son, the book on her 80th birthday in 2014. While Brian will always keep the original book as a family heirloom he felt it should be published so that a wider public could enjoy its contents.

Margaret enjoying the Devon countryside

Honiton

Ottery
St Mary

Sidbury

East Devon Way

The Commons

Newton
Poppleford

South Wes

Sidmouth

Budleigh
Salterton

Exmouth

East Devon
Area of Outstanding Natural Beauty

Courtesy East Devon Area of Outstanding Natural Beauty and the artist Peter Lightfoot.

NATURE NOTES: DONALD CAMPBELL

Devon Lane

Although *My Devonshire Year* tells of times long gone, the experiences that Margaret valued so much, like the seasonal sequence of hedge bank flowers, are still there to be enjoyed.

Margaret describes the ducks on Combpyne '*Harbour*' on 28th February reminding me of living across the road, seeing many more Moorhens than ducks and of the Spring flowers along the lanes towards Boshill Cross. Despite the damage to roadside banks by huge tractor wheels it is still '*difficult to surpass the Devon hedgerows in May and June*' (her journal 3rd June). One gain, since Margaret's year of 1979, has been the creation of Lower Bruckland Ponds, near Boshill, and their colonisation by dragonflies.

SEATON WETLANDS

Floods at Seaton

The January journal tells of floods, ever changing weather and calling Curlew around the estuary of the Axe. It only hints at the bird life but later in the year on 12th October the whole of the mudflats were closely dotted with flocks of birds while on 12th January Margaret mentions four of the most characteristic birds of the Wetlands. In recent years bird ringers have demonstrated that Wigeon will fly 2,500 miles between the Axe and Russia several times in their lives. They have also tried to unravel the complexity of the lives and movements of the Shelduck. Oyster Catchers now breed on the islands in Black Hole Marsh and still gather '*in the field opposite Axmouth Bridge*' (4th March). The marshes on the other side of the river provide one of the few breeding sites for Devon Redshank. Margaret mentions Cuckoos, Skylarks and Swifts which have all greatly decreased but Little Egrets have arrived to breed and there are good numbers of Black-tailed Godwits. Ospreys, Mediterranean Gulls and Cetti's Warblers visit regularly and 212 species were recorded within 3 miles of Axmouth Bridge in 2007; these included national rarities. More birdwatchers, more species and more creative management for birds and for people are all thanks to the East Devon Countryside Service and their volunteers. The best way to see the changes around the Axe is to travel by the tramline which reached Colyton in 1980.

AXMOUTH TO LYME REGIS UNDERCLIFFS

Nightingales can no longer be heard in the National Nature Reserve but Peregrines, following pesticide deaths and egg thinning, have increased along Devon coasts and like Marsh Tit, Bullfinch and Blackcap do well in the Undercliffs. Margaret's journal tells of going to The Slabs, the Jurassic rocks closest to Seaton, on the 27th August. Walking over awkward boulders and tiring shingle she noted Purple Loosestrife at Culverhole where it still grows. Her objective was the Brixham trawler *Fairway* which had run aground on the 2nd December. It was later to be blown up, its remains left to rust and gradually

decay, along with a digger which had optimistically been driven from Seaton in the hope of salvage. Apart from the trawler she found that '*water... cascaded over the slabs of Blue Lias and collected in crystal clear pools*'. It does just the same today.

Pinhay Beach

Later Margaret walked the length of the Reserve stopping at '*the famous landmark*' of Landslip Cottage. Despite what she wrote on the 13th September there are still the remains of walls and an assortment of kitchen detritus while nearby the sheep wash, built in 1800, has been restored and maintained by Natural England and volunteers. Its size implies a large local sheep population while the fact that it is now surrounded by mature trees emphasise how much things can change.

In November, walking with friends, she had to negotiate fallen trees on the path, as can happen today, before taking '*the rough steps down to Pinhay Bay*'. Here they had a problem with a large spectacular Ammonite; should they rescue it or abandon it to the sea? There are still different views about the collection of fossils but there is no doubt that if left most will be lost to the sea. The rough steps are now gone.

Margaret did not go to the rich chalk grasslands of the Undercliffs where eleven species of orchid grow and tiny lime loving plants like Squinancywort, Fairy Flax, Autumn Gentian, Wild Thyme and Rockrose do well nor, I suspect, would she have wanted to explore the soft eroding cliffs colonised by specialist sun loving invertebrates. A brief survey in 2003 found sixty endangered or nationally rare species and a '*bioblitz*' ten years later identified 186 fly species and 252 moths in one day.

WEST TO BRANSCOMBE

Snakelocks Anemone

As the chalk extends West the grassland plant community does likewise. Its composition, as shown by atlases of plant distribution from different dates, changes little over time in contrast the butterfly species that have not survived so well. Nottingham Catchfly is a rare plant that Margaret illustrates in her June chapter. Like Purple Gromwell, conspicuous by the coast path in The Underhooken it has a very limited national distribution. Margaret noted five thistle species near Boshill but nine can be found around Beer Head.

She often compares White Cliff, West of Seaton, to Haven Cliff to the East, for with both visible from her flat she could watch the light changing throughout the day whether in sunshine or in mist. A landslip on White Cliff on New Year's Day 1979, was only one of many before and since with a dramatic one closing the steps to Seaton Hole in 2000 and a more recent one leading to the abandonment of the Old Beer Road.

On the 9th October Margaret took the challenging route along the beach East from Beer when she found '*interesting things in rock pools*' and saw a Shag diving. Shags and Peregrines sometimes, and Jackdaws, Cormorants, Ravens and Fulmars more often, nest on the cliffs. In the rock pools Beadlet, Strawberry and Snakelocks Anemones' and a wide variety of Crabs and other crustaceans, occur along with Sea Hares, purple – brown sea slugs with ear like appendages and Worm Pipe – fish which look like lengths of discarded boot laces. The Fine Foundation Heritage Centre often organise rock pooling sessions on the equally productive Beer Beach.

CRABBING IN LYME BAY

On the 17th June Margaret went South into Lyme Bay sitting '*on the fore cubby as the pots were hauled*.' The boat passed Finger and Thumb, an important Haven Cliff landmark, partnered since May 2014, by the remains of another landslip slightly further East. Five Lobsters, three large crabs and numerous Spider crabs were the haul when she returned to Axmouth. A fortnight later she was out again '*looking down into the clear green water to another world*'. At that time it was a world little known but

Lobster and Edible Crab

since explored by many divers, damaged by scallopers and others and investigated, with a view to protection, by Devon Wildlife Trust and Plymouth University. As always Margaret was fascinated by colour '*with burnt umber and dark green ribbons*' in that other world of changing moods which she had only observed from land. Some of the effects of these moods were to change late in 1979 when work started on what has, ever since, been a controversial sea defence scheme along the Seaton sea front.

STORMS, VIEWS AND CONSERVATION INITIATIVES

**Devon patchwork,
View from Trow Hill**

Margaret's year began and ended with storms for on the 4th January '*massive seas crashed against Beer Head*' and on 27th December the Axe Valley '*was like a huge lake*'. On 13th February when Portland experienced high tides and freak waves Seaton suffered '*utter devastation along the sea front*'. Inland, snow in Colyton '*settled on the roofs of houses like a thick frost*' as late as 2nd May but it was back to the coast in August when '*furious seas lashed the beach all day causing fifteen to drown in the Fastnet Yacht Race early on the 14th.*'

Storms produce their own fine views but Margaret described and illustrated others on '*ordinary*' walks and on '*excursions*'. One of the former was from the cliff at Branscombe on 29th September and the latter included the view of the Fleet from above Abbotsbury (11th August), looking over the Exe to distant Dartmoor *(20th September)* and across the East Devon Area of Outstanding Natural Beauty from Trow Hill *(26th April)* near the site of the now highly popular Donkey Sanctuary.

For further information on the following conservation organizations please visit their websites:

AVDCS
www.axevaleconservation.org.uk

Devon Wildlife Trust
www.devonwildlifetrust.org

East Devon AONB Partnership
www.aonb.org.uk

East Devon Countryside Service
www.eastdevon.gov.uk/countryside

Jurassic Coast WHS
www.jurassiccoast.com

National Trust
www.nationaltrust.org

Natural England
www.naturalengland.com

Seaton Jurassic
www.seatonjurassic.org

SVCT
www.seatonvisitorcentretrust.org

These views, like much described in *My Devonshire Year* remain spectacular, helped by many groups and individuals. Beautiful views and diverse wildlife are vital to the local economy and are the concern of the East Devon AONB Partnership whilst the East Devon Countryside Service has established Local Nature Reserves, notably the Seaton Wetlands. Natural England and the National Trust work to maintain coastal habitats while the whole Dorset and East Devon coast has become England's only natural World Heritage site. Devon Wildlife Trust and the District and County Councils are establishing Seaton Jurassic which interprets the local coast and its history in the context of evolution. The Centre is not far from where Margaret and Brian watched the changing light on Haven Cliff some forty years ago.

DONALD CAMPBELL

In 1993 Donald retired early from his role as Senior Tutor in a Sixth Form College. Once in Devon he became an enthusiast for the Undercliffs and for counting birds there and around the Axe Wetlands as part of national surveys. To his surprise this enthusiasm led to his election of Chairman of the Axe Vale and District Conservation Society and after twelve years in that role he became President in 2008. As Chairman and President he was a member of the East Devon AONB Partnership of which he became Chairman in 2009. He has been a Trustee of Holyford Woodland Trust for many years and of Seaton Visitor Centre since 2007. The Trust works closely with Devon Wildlife Trust and East Devon District Council in establishing the new Seaton Jurassic Centre.

ACKNOWLEDGEMENTS

In alphabetical order by surname:

Donald Campbell, Trustee of the Jurassic Centre, Seaton for his informative and interesting Nature Notes article, **Mark Couch** at SRP, Exeter for their excellent printing, **Laurence Daeche** for his talented design and production skills, **David Knight** and all at Tormark for their important sales and distribution services, **Jon Robinson-Pratt** for his meticulous photography, **Richard Webb** for his encouragement and for contributing his publishing expertise, **Daniel Williams** at the Met Office, Exeter for comparative weather information and **Pete Youngman** at the East Devon AONB for the use of their helpful map. Finally, to my wife **Julie** for her important support and involvement, and to my **Mother** without whom neither I nor the book would exist…! My thanks to you all for your important contributions to the publication of *My Devonshire Year*.   **Brian Pogson**

THE PUBLISHER: RICHARD WEBB

After over 50 years in publishing I retired in 2014 but a chance enquiry from Brian Pogson and the first sight of his mother's beautiful manuscript quickly changed my mind..!

I was educated at Marlborough College and the London College of Communication. I started my career in 1961 in Fleet Street at Hulton Press and then Condé Nast Publications (VOGUE and HOUSE & GARDEN) publishing amongst other books *Goodbye, Baby & Amen* by David Bailey.

I then became Publicity Director of Michael Joseph Publishers and promoted the work of James Baldwin, H.E. Bates, Dick Francis, James Herriot, John Masters, Spike Milligan, Derek Tangye, Leslie Thomas and Harold Wilson amongst many others. I finally left London to become Publicity Director of David & Charles back in Devon.

In 1975 I co-founded Webb & Bower, Publishers in Exeter and we published 333 titles including 24 national bestsellers and one international bestseller. Webb & Bower received 14 publishing awards for design, typography and production and had 13 books or series that sold over 100,000 copies worldwide.

The Country Diary of an Edwardian Lady by Edith Holden was published by us in 1977 and received a Gold Plaque for the first million copies sold. The book has now sold over three million copies in 13 languages. It achieved an entry in the *Guinness Book of Records* for the longest-running No.1 bestseller and in 2014 to celebrate *The Sunday Times Bestsellers List's* 40th anniversary *The Country Diary of an Edwardian Lady* was declared the fourth national bestselling title over the last 40 years.

I later moved from Exeter to Dartmouth, where my family have lived for nearly a century, and became a local publisher. In 2000 *The Chronicles of Dartmouth* was published which won the *Devon Book of the Year Award*. Since then I have published a dozen books on Dartmouth and South Devon including an acclaimed history of the Britannia Royal Naval College.

My Devonshire Year ranks with the finest books that I have ever published and, with my own love of Devon, it is the perfect swan song to my long publishing career.   **Richard Webb**

PUBLISHER'S NOTE
Margaret I. Pogson's original manuscript has been typeset exactly as it was written and without any changes. Her grammar and spelling was so good that none were needed. We have kept her capitalization of the initial letter of flora and fauna as it is her style. The only addition we have made to the text has been to insert a cross-reference to the nearest relevant illustration for the ease and enjoyment of the reader.

DISCLAIMER

MY
DEVONSHIRE
YEAR

1979

Margaret J. Pogson.

January

Silvery ferns on frosted windows,
Icicles hang from the sill,
Drifting snow in frozen furrows,
All around is quiet and still.

Margaret I. Pogson

Snow on Seaton Marshes *(see 24th Jan.)*

JANUARY

NEW YEAR DAWNS

1st Jan. The New Year dawned with the glow of a golden and red sunrise on windows thickly frosted with silvery ferns and wisps of white mist drifting over the surface of the sea. At 8.30 a.m. I walked along the Esplanade but could barely see the waves breaking on the shore for the dense clouds of mist rising from the water. As each wave receded, the beach was left steaming in the frosty air. Even the gulls huddled dejectedly in a group. No more snow has fallen since the heavy blizzard on the 30th Dec. but the roads are rutted with frozen snow and packed ice in sharp ridges. In the afternoon I returned home along the Marsh path. The snow was beginning to melt in the warm sunshine and most had gone from the church roof but the air was still frosty. Everywhere was quiet and still and the distant snow-covered hills were beautiful in the afternoon sunlight. Only the startled flutter of a disturbed black-bird broke the silence.

Ivy *(see 21st Jan.)*

2ⁿᵈ Jan. A crisp, cold morning with a golden and pink sunrise against the clear blue-green sky. Temperatures must have risen during the night as the frosty patterns that formed on the windows early yesterday evening had almost thawed completely when I got up at 6.40am, and yet the minimum temperature for the night read only 5°F. Warm sunshine and clear blue sky all day but the snow remained hard underfoot and it wasn't until late afternoon the packed ice on the roads began to thaw. I went to look for Teasels *(see page 11)* on the path by Roman Way. How the snow had transformed the drab hedgerows, silhouetting the dried seed-heads of Cow Parsley, Dock, Campion *(see page 11)* and Tansy *(see page 13)*. The papery clusters of Maple wings *(see page 169)* still hung from the trees and fat red rose-hips added a brilliant splash of colour. I found a large Teasel with at least a dozen and a half heads and carried home an armful of the things I had collected. Despite the lack of colour, they really are quite beautiful, such shapes and forms and fine delicate outlines. The sea is calm today but all the recent storms have left large areas of sand.

3ʳᵈ Jan. A cold grey morning but at least the thaw has set in. The bay is one mass of white-crested brown-grey seas swept in all day by freshening SSE winds.

4ᵗʰ Jan. Strong SE winds to gale force and huge waves rolling in 10-15 ft. high. I watched as massive seas crashed against Beer Head, the flying white-water and spray reaching up into the foliage above the chalk cliffs.

Nipplewort
(see 21st Jan.)

Dock
(see 21st Jan.)

5th Jan. A pale golden morning followed by hazy sunshine all day but a strong, bitterly cold wind. The sun set over Beer Head a brilliant orange and pink against the clear blue and jade green sky of a frosty evening twinkling with stars. *(see pages 16/17).*

FROZEN RIVER AND ICE FLOES

6th Jan. A particularly beautiful sunrise this morning. Orange and pink clouds in a pale green sky, to the East, gradually shading to pink clouds in a blue sky to the West. The Axe was frozen over again this morning but it had thawed by early afternoon and large ice floes were drifting down river with the ebbing tide *(see page 13).* As the water receded great sheets of ice were left on the mud-flats and along the banks there still remained much snow. A Cormorant dived repeatedly as Shelducks, Gulls and Common Sandpipers fed at the water's edge and the plaintive cry of a Curlew echoed across the valley *(see pages 14/15).* Large areas of the higher marshes are still frozen with flood water and from Boshill the landscape was wild and wintry, fields mottled with the remaining snow fading into misty blue distances.

Storm-lashed Beer Head *(see 4th Jan.)*

Low Tide on the Axe *(see 28th Jan.)*

7ᵗʰ Jan. A damp, grey morning with heavy cloud obliterating the cliff-tops and drizzle in the air. I enjoyed an early morning walk along the sea-front – a firmness underfoot, as overnight much of the snow and ice had disappeared, and an exhilarating freshness without the icy sting of recent weather.

9ᵗʰ Jan. Another lovely fresh morning, bathed in pale wintry sunlight. The undulating coastline to Start Point was clearly visible, an ominous sign of bad weather which proved correct as by evening it was raining and strong winds became gale force.

10ᵗʰ Jan. A terrific storm last night, one of the worst I can remember. The roar of the sea, howling gales and the rain lashing on the window kept waking me and at 1 a.m. I got up to put dust sheets beneath the windows and mop up the water forced in by the wind. By morning it had abated somewhat and the sea was steadily rolling in with long straight waves, white-crests sparkling in the sunlight. By midday the wind had freshened again bringing heavy cloud, thunder and lightning and a fierce hailstorm. Heavy rainstorms continued throughout the afternoon but by late evening the sky cleared, leaving a frosty moonlit night.

Tree fungi
(see 15th July)

11ᵗʰ Jan. There appears to have been a rock-fall to the right of White Cliff as from our window this morning I could see a fan-shaped area of earth and rocks on the beach by Seaton Hole.

12ᵗʰ Jan. Early this morning the sun was filtering down through the dark clouds on to the sea in great shafts of light, a truly magnificent sight. Later the clouds merged, but somewhere the sun broke through illuminating one solitary headland by White Cliff, golden, whilst the rest of the coastline remained shaded and sombre. We went to Seaton Hole in the afternoon and found the beach covered with huge boulders, much rock and clay, where part of the cliff had fallen. Large areas of chalk are exposed and many cracks appearing. I am sure more will fall before the end of the Winter. A perky little Robin, all fluffed up to keep himself warm, hopped from rock to rock *(see page 9)* and as we walked back up the path we could see a Great Spotted Woodpecker in the trees at the top *(see page 18)*. As the tide was out, we decided to go to the Axe to watch the birds on the mud-flats *(see pages 6/7)*. There were Curlews with long curved bills, chestnut-headed Widgeon and the little Sandpipers scurrying about, their heads a bobbing as they searched for food, Oystercatchers and one or two Redshanks with their bright legs. All these and the usual Gulls and Crows busily occupied at the water's edge. One bird dived repeatedly, staying under water for some time before re-emerging. I couldn't identify it, although it was very dark in colour and appeared to be one of the duck family. It certainly wasn't a Cormorant or Shag *(see page 15)*.

15th Jan. A very mild, grey morning with heavy cloud to the West and drizzle in the air. The sea was very still, barely turning on the shore, the light ripples scalloping the beach with miniature inlets. For one short moment during the morning there must have been a break in the clouds as the dark sea was lit with a shimmering patch of pure silver light. I think more of the cliff has fallen as there appears to be more rubble on the beach, to the left of the first lot.

A SPECTACULAR SUNSET

16th Jan. A most spectacular sunset, dark clouds illuminated with red and gold against a sky fading from gold and green to pink and violet on the horizon.

17th Jan. A glowing golden sunrise from behind dark clouds against a sky of turquoise and blue. A strong cold wind from the North blew ripples away from the shore, keeping the sea unnaturally still. By mid-morning the wind had freshened bringing flurries of snow which settled but on the lower ground it soon turned to rain. Evening brought more snow from the East and we wonder what it will be like in the morning.

Rock-hopping Robin
(see 12th Jan.)

Fleabane
(see 19th Aug.)

Mugwort
(see 5th Sept.)

Greater Bindweed
(see 21st Jan.)

Burdock
(see 17th July.)

Cow Parsley
and
Campion
(see 2nd Jan.)

Teasels
(see 2nd Jan.)

18th Jan. A bitterly cold, grey day. No more snow during the night but all around us it still lingers on the hills and cliffs, usually a sign of more to come. Rough seas and white horses all across the bay.

19th Jan. Another dull, grey morning with dark threatening clouds. At 9 a.m. it suddenly began to snow heavily and continued all the morning until it was 2-3ins. deep and drifting in places. However at 1 p.m. it gradually turned to rain and by late afternoon the snow had completely disappeared.

20th Jan. A myriad of effects of light and cloud over the sea this morning – a constantly changing show of form and colour. The heavy rain and melting snow has resulted in the usual flooding of the marshes at this time of year. I heard today that the cliff fall *(see page 27)* I first noticed on 11th January actually happened on New Year's Eve. In consequence the path to Beer is closed as part of it is now on the cliff edge.

PERFECT REFLECTIONS

21st Jan. A hard frost last night and a crisp, clear morning with a very high tide. The river was a wide expanse of quiet, still water, not a single ripple disturbed the perfect reflections on its glassy surface. Later a crow caused quite a commotion splashing about at the water's edge enjoying his morning bathe. The floods have receded but there are still large areas of water in the fields by the river and drifts of snow at Rousdon. I went along the Marsh path and over the rough ground nearby, looking for seed-heads to paint. Everything is very dead, the severe frosts and snow having taken their toll and the plants remain dormant. I found the dry twisted stems of Greater Bindweed *(see page 10)* with some seed-pods still attached and could hear the seeds rattling inside. Picked a handful of various plants and what had singularly looked so lifeless became quite attractive when complemented by another, the pale, papery Nipplewort *(see pages 4 and 126)* and red-brown Dock *(see page 4)* with the glossy dark-green leaves of the Ivy *(see page 3)*.

23rd Jan. Yesterday's rain and sleet turned to snow during the night and this morning we looked out to find everything covered with a soft white blanket 2-3ins. deep. Heavy cloud threatened more snow and it remained bitterly cold all day. The sea was grey and still as though numbed by the bleakness of the weather.

The Axe Estuary & Haven Cliff *(see 6th Jan.)*

13

24th Jan. A very hard frost last
night and patterns on the windows
this morning. Some of the roads
are like ice-rinks. Saw four
swans take-off from the river, necks
outstretched, wings slowly but powerfully
beating and webbed feet as though
running on the water – then gradual take-
off, a magnificent sight. Gradually gaining
in height and flying in formation, they
turned away from the river and slowly
disappeared from view. From the
Colyford Bridge we looked out across
the snow-covered marshes to Seaton
(see page 2), the buildings on the sea-front
a dark blue-grey silhouette against the misty
peach-pink sky of a wintry afternoon. Before
returning home I walked to the end of the track
to the marshes to see if there was much snow and
found lots of small footprints, rabbits', birds' and two
other tiny creatures. Next time I must make a sketch
of them so they can be identified. Goldfinches were
busy amongst some seed-heads, flashes of brilliant colour

Tansy
(see 2nd Jan.)

Wood Sage
(see 29th July.)

against the snow. A cold, misty stillness settled over the countryside as the light began to fade and we hurried home to the warmth of the fireside.

27th Jan. A second day of brilliant sunshine from a clear blue sky from first thing in the morning until sunset but very cold.

Key to Birds on the Axe *(see 12th Jan.)*

1. Crow	7. Curlew	13. Oystercatcher
2. Shelduck	8. Great Black-Backed Gull	14. Dunlin
3. Mute Swan	9. Common Sandpiper	15. Widgeon
4. Little Grebe	10. Black-Headed Gull	16. Heron
5. Lapwing	11. Redshank	17. Cormorant
6. Ringed Plover	12. Mallard	18. Herring Gulls

Winter Sunset – Beer Head *(see 5th Jan.)*

**Greater Spotted
Woodpecker**
(see 12th Jan.)

CLOUDS OF PEACH AND GOLD

28th Jan. A beautiful clear morning after a hard frost last night. Some of the fields by the Axe are still flooded, frozen and edged with snow *(see pages 6/7)*. From Boshill we could see the snow still lying on all the high ground but just odd fields were completely white. The colours of the countryside were so beautiful today – subdued by Winter but clear and subtle. The distant blues of the cliffs behind Lyme Regis, the mottled red of ploughed fields dusted with snow and the stark contrast of bare trees. Near Rousdon there was a field of ewes with their lambs – such a shame for them to be born so early, before the milder Spring weather is here. The wind freshened by noon and the sea was wild and stormy, with heavy rain turning to ice in the evening. Along the horizon by Start Point there were the most beautiful clouds of peach and gold glowing bright and clear beyond the dark night sky.

30th Jan. Today was mild and sunny with a gentle hint of Spring in the air but there are still patches of snow amongst the long grass and in sheltered hollows on the high ground. The birds are very hungry and great numbers soon congregate when food is put out for them.

Magpie
(see 28th Feb.)

February

Frozen puddles slowly thawing,
Thick grey mist and drizzly rain,
Shepherds busy with the lambing,
Snowdrops growing in the lane.

Margaret I. Pogson

Haven Cliff – Early morning *(see 11th Feb.)*

FEBRUARY

THE ROAR OF THE WAVES

1st Feb. I awoke at 6.15 a.m. and lay in bed listening to the rain beating on the window and the sound of the sea – the roar of the waves on the shore and the hiss of the shingle swept down the beach by the returning water. When I left for Lincolnshire at 7.45 a.m. great waves were breaking in flurries of spray and the tide was running high along the Axe with much flooding in the fields *(see page 32)*. Such a miserable journey with heavy cloud and rain until I reached Peterborough, where I noticed the first snow. From then on we ran into blizzards and soon the train was speeding through the snow-covered countryside. As I trundled along the little branch-line to the coast, the snow gradually disappeared leaving frozen gravel pits and the bleak, wintry Fenland scene.

5th Feb. Home again tomorrow and how much I look forward to it. There has been some sunshine but mostly very dull with icy winds that seem to steal through one.

6th Feb. There was a severe hoar-frost when I left Lincolnshire this morning and thick fog away from the coast. From Peterborough to London it was sunny but as I travelled Westward it began to rain and by early evening, when I arrived at Axminster Station, it was torrential. It glistened in the station lights as it bounced off the dark windswept platform.

7th Feb. Heavy cloud over the cliffs and much rain all day.

Gorse *(see 23rd Feb.)*

21

The Floods at Seaton on 13th February *(see 13th Feb.)*

10th Feb. A dreary, wet day so typical of February. There is snow about 1-2 ins. Deep on Honiton Common but no sign of it here – yet!

11th Feb. Haven Cliff and the cliffs beyond just a blur of misty-grey this morning *(see page 20)*. Cold, damp and depressing all day, turning even colder in the evening.

12th Feb. About an inch of snow fell during the night and more fine powdery flakes all the morning, at mid-day it turned to rain and by the middle of the afternoon the snow here had melted away. Long, steady waves with sinister dark crests rolling slowly in breaking thunderously and sweeping up the beach in masses of white foam.

STORM AND FLOODS

13th Feb. We were suddenly awoken at 5.45 a.m. and looked out to find utter devastation along the sea-front *(see page 22)*. Huge waves were breaking over the sea-wall, sweeping across the road and cascading over the garden walls. The Esplanade was one swirling mass of debris and dirty, brown water often topped 3 feet high by the banks of shingle swept in by the flood. Terrific waves hurled spray skywards and as they crashed down in a wall of water the vibration could be felt throughout the building. The front door was broken down by the weight of the water swirling in shoulder-high and the front gates and letter-box in the porch washed away by the torrent that swept through the bottom flat. This continued until well past 10 a.m. No storm, no warning – just huge waves with dark, straight crests rolling mercilessly in. A light wind from the North and much rain for most of the day adding to the discomfort and despair of the residents salvaging the remains of their flooded homes. Despite warnings of worse conditions on the evening tide and advised to evacuate our home, we decided to stay and it passed without incident, just reaching the sea wall and splashing over a couple of times.

Last Year's Beech Leaves

14th Feb. The sea came over only slightly this morning, the strong winds from the North blowing the water away from the shore in an eerie backward movement. The ferocity of the sea yesterday has left large areas of sand on the beach again but today it has returned to its more usual wintry composure with only faint traces of the heavy swell. It turned much colder during the day and by late afternoon the sky looked heavy with snow, dark clouds silhouetted against a golden sunset. The high bank of shingle between the estuary and the sea was breached in several places yesterday, the hollows clearly visible where the water had swept through.

15th Feb. A severe frost this morning with small patches of light snow and a strong bitterly cold wind bringing more flurries in the evening but at least we had some sunshine during the day. By early evening the windows were beginning to get their frosty patterns and the moon shone brilliantly in a clear sky.

16th Feb. A light covering of snow this morning and odd rain and snow showers. The cold North wind of yesterday had abated so it felt much milder and the sea was quiet and placid – a certain calmness after all the turmoil of the past few days. I read today that at one time during the high water on Tuesday the Axe was blocked by the shingle washed from the sea-bank into the river and that one square mile of Seaton was flooded up to 4 feet deep.

FLOODED MARSHES

17th Feb. For days now the flooded marshes have been frozen and white with a covering of snow. We hear of severe weather on the East coast with many villages and large towns cut off by huge drifts. How we shall appreciate the coming of Spring this year after such a long, hard Winter.

18th Feb. Thick fog and rain for most of the day, so dreary and dismal but much milder. On the way to Uplyme they were busy ploughing *(see pages 30/31)*, beautiful red furrows on the curve of the hill dotted white with hungry Seagulls. We had to wait whilst a shepherd gathered his flock together and moved them off jostling along the road – a large ram with majestic spiralled horns, ewes and fat woolly lambs *(see page 19)*.

**Young Hazel
Catkins, Ash Twigs
and Snowdrops**
(see 28th Feb.)

22nd Feb. A pale misty-grey morning with just a hint of brightness but it was soon evident that it was going to be a beautiful day as the sky softened to blue and the sun broke through. At last a break from all the depressing weather and a hint of Spring. We walked to the mouth of the Axe where the river had become quite narrow and appeared shallow enough to paddle across but the tide was ebbing and the current strong. A bulldozer and mechanical digger were busy removing the shingle from the river and re-building the bank lowered by the sea during the floods on the 13th. Part of Haven Cliff was quite clear of foliage and had obviously fallen and been washed away. We noticed the buds on the trees were beginning to swell.

WOODBURY COMMON

23rd Feb. Picnicked on Woodbury Common today. Everywhere was bathed in brilliant sunshine but the wind was cold. We could see the pale silvery waters of the Exe and beyond to Dartmoor and in the far distance to the right, the shimmering brilliance of the sea on the curve of the bay to Dawlish and Teignmouth. Behind us the hills, patterned with fields and the common land of the coastline between Sidmouth and Budleigh Salterton, brown dead bracken, rich green conifers and the pinky haze of bare twigs and buds about to burst. In a few sheltered places the Gorse is still flowering *(see page 21)* but most look quite battered by the weather. A beautiful day and such a joy to feel the warmth of the sun and see countryside begin to come alive again. On the way home we stopped above the old Beer Road to look out across Seaton Bay to Haven Cliff and Culverhole Point.

Hart's Tongue Fern

The Cliff-fall at Seaton Hole *(see 20th Jan.)*

27

24th Feb. Woke to hear the gentle sound of the sea and the lone cry of a Curlew and watched as the light brightened through the curtains promising another glorious day. The Herring Gulls are back on the roof, or Mr & Mrs Seagull as we more affectionately refer to them *(see page 37)*. They have been with us since we first moved in over eight years ago but usually remained during the Winter months, often coming to be fed. At the end of last Summer they suddenly disappeared – perhaps they were aware of the severe weather to come and decided to find a more sheltered abode.

RELUCTANT MOTHER NATURE

25th Feb. Heard the Curlew again this morning – a pale blue misty morning with warm golden sunshine but a very severe frost which persisted until late, in the shady places. All the colours of the countryside still belong to February despite the beautiful weather. Mother Nature somehow seems reluctant to show herself and the bright sunlight accentuates the deadness of everything. No Snowdrops, no Lambs' Tails, no birds busy making nests – maybe a sign there is still more severe weather to come. The trees are beautiful outlines of grey-green silhouetted in the sunlight against the bare countryside and casting long dark shadows.

26th Feb. Thick fog and a severe hoar frost this morning. It was mid-day before it cleared and even then remains of it could be seen drifting along the Axe valley. Brilliant sunshine and a clear blue sky for the rest of the day but a chill in the air. The sea has again made little inlets all along the beach, scalloping the edge.

27th Feb. There were pools all along the beach this morning where the sea had come over the ridge and it turned stormy as the S.W. winds freshened during the day but the high Spring tide passed without event. However, there are warnings that the sea may be over tomorrow morning so we are setting the alarm for at least an hour before high tide at 7 a.m.

Ivy Berries

Preparing to plough *(see 18th Feb.)*

PROMISE OF SPRING

28th Feb. The storm heightened during the night but when we awoke this morning we could tell there was no cause for alarm as the wind had dropped and the sea had returned to its more majestic fervour. The last day of the month and a promise of Spring to come. We drove to Uplyme through the narrow lanes of Combpyne, Shapwick and Venlake, stopping, as always, at Combpyne 'Harbour' to look at the ducks. They were enjoying a siesta in the afternoon sunshine and by their agitated quacks made it quite clear they didn't like being disturbed. The first wild Snowdrops are out in the hedge by Clock House *(see page 25)* and on the roadside just past the old station where a startled Magpie *(see page 18)* flew up from the road. Through Shapwick the sheep were grazing on the steep grassy fields and by Cannington Viaduct some inquisitive little lambs with black faces and legs came skipping to the gate and peered through as we passed. I picked the first Lambs' Tails, so late this year, and some Ash Twigs with fat black buds *(see page 25)*, but there is no sign yet of the Lesser Periwinkle which normally would be carpeting the bank under the hedgerows by waterside. The spikes of Lords and Ladies have grown quite rapidly during the sunshine of the last few days and are easily discernible owing to the lack of other greenery.

Floods in the Axe Valley *(see 1st Feb.)*

March

Weather changes as it pleases,
Mild and sunny, bleak and chill,
Blustering winds and gentle breezes,
Stir the golden daffodil.

Margaret I. Pogson

Whitford Weir *(see 22nd June)*

MARCH

IN LIKE A LAMB

1st March. The month came in like a lamb, mild with some sunshine but clouding over later and a calm, grey sea.

3rd March. Heavy mist over the cliffs and light drizzle for most of the day.

4th March. A beautiful, mild still morning with the sunlight softly breaking through. As the mud-flats were covered by the high tide, a large number of Oystercatchers were feeding in the corner of the field opposite the Axe bridge. Sunshine, broken with cloud, all day turning much colder in the evening with a clear moonlit sky and brightly twinkling stars promising frost.

6th March. White horses sweeping in on dark, steely-grey seas, their foaming crests catching the pale early morning light. Stormy and rough with gale force winds followed by heavy cloud and lashing rain in the afternoon. Much colder.

7th March. A beautiful deep blue and white sea this morning all ragged waves and white horses but by 10 a.m. it had become calm and was quite grey. Sunshine and heavy showers all day with snow at Honiton but a dark threatening cloud here slowly passed over.

Bracket Fungi

South Combe Higher Barn

8th March. A bright, clear, sunny morning but soon the wind freshened and heavy cloud rolled in from the sea. In the lanes between Axmouth and Dowlands it was quite still and mild, pale sunlight intermittently breaking through the clouds. As we sat painting, a Lark hovered high in the sky, trilling his merry song.

9th March. Sunshine and heavy showers for most of the day and a beautiful rainbow over the marshes *(see page 40)*. Bright clear moonlit night.

10th March. A thoroughly soggy wet day. Between the showers I walked part of the way along the Marsh Path trying to avoid the mud but not minding the puddles. The air was fresh and clear but otherwise there was little pleasure in being out of doors as everything is still so dead with few signs of life to hint of Spring around the corner.

MR & MRS SEAGULL

12th March. Sunny and mild. Mr & Mrs Seagull appear to have taken up their Summer residence again amongst the chimney-pots *(see below and page 67)* and are up to their usual tricks, tapping on the windows and the porch door and flying down to keep me company whenever I am on the roof. Whilst I was downstairs for a few moments this morning, they scattered the pegs and washing all over the place in their search for food. When we first moved into the flat they wheeled and dived, screeching around our heads, each time we set foot on the roof and I soon realised there would not be any peace until I claimed my own territory. So on the next occasion, instead of retreating to the safety of the porch, I stood my ground and raising my arms flapped madly around the roof after them, squawking raucously. I had to repeat this somewhat hilarious spectacle a couple of times before there was an uneasy truce, but after that it did not take long to gain their confidence and we were soon happily sharing the roof together. However, it was some years before they would accept the less familiar members of the family.

Mr & Mrs Seagull *(see 24th Feb./12th March)*

Haven Cliff to Culverhole Point *(see 13th March)*

13th March. As I walked home along the sea-front this morning, Haven Cliff *(see page 38)* was stark against a leaden sky but as I watched, a thick grey cloud moving slowly from the North reached the cliff edge but instead of continuing horizontally it drifted silently downwards until the cliff-face was obliterated by an eerie blanket of mist.

14th March. The first of the March winds. When I woke this morning I could hear it blustering in the porch. Windy and very wet all day with heavy snow and sleet at times and much colder. Will this long dreary Winter never end!

BLIZZARDS

15th March. Bitterly cold with heavy blizzards on high ground but none settled. We drove through the narrow lanes to Southleigh and Colyton and saw the first primroses of the year by the stream at Kilmington but otherwise there was little sign of life in the hedgerows.

16th March. In the pale blue-grey light of early morning I could see a circle of gulls bathing and feeding just off-shore in a pool of shimmering silver sea. It was enough to make one shiver to see them on such a cold morning with more snow on the high ground around us overnight. The sun broke through for a short while during the afternoon but by evening it was raining again.

Rain over Axmouth *(see 9th March)*

The Axe Estuary *(see 17th March)*

41

17th March. A beautiful sunny morning with the sea as calm and still as a mill-pond but a chill in the air. More snow on the high ground around us and inland but once again Seaton has escaped it. I walked to the mouth of the Axe in the late afternoon, to sketch. The tide was ebbing and the river running fast, causing much disturbance in the water where it flowed over rocks and boulders, making it sound more like a moorland stream *(see page 41)*.

18th March. Rain and blizzards this morning and although it didn't settle locally, the high ground was covered with snow. From Boshill we could see the white fields on all the hill tops and there was a light covering at Rousdon. The sun broke through by early afternoon but the weather remained unsettled for the rest of the day.

HAIL STORMS

21st March. Clear blue sky and brilliant sunshine from early morning but by noon heavy cloud had formed and soon there were severe hail storms. Sunshine and heavy showers for the rest of the day and a much colder evening.

22nd March. A very mild sunny morning giving way to short, sharp showers. In the afternoon the effects of light and cloud were spectacular. Blue sky overhead with great dark grey clouds against a thick misty blanket, its edge clear-cut in the far distance, revealing brilliant billowing golden clouds on the horizon, against the sombre blue of the hills. Here and there a field shone bright with colour, picked out by a stray patch of sunlight. Towards early evening, although there was not a spectacular sunset, the clouds, all around the whole circumference of the horizon were warm grey tinged with pink.

23rd March. Very severe frost last night but a beautiful clear sunny day from sunrise to sunset and bright twinkling stars at night.

24th March. Dull and cold with rain by late afternoon and strengthening winds making for a rough, stormy night.

25th March. Much heavy cloud and misty rain obliterating the cliffs. Stormy brown seas and dirty brown foam blowing up the beach. The water came over the ridge making a long canal but the Force 8 gale abated before high tide. However, the evening remained stormy and the wind freshened again to gale force, a pale gleaming sunset catching the crests of the waves as they majestically swept in.

26th March. Much calmer by morning and turning colder with some hail today.

ROLLING BREAKERS

27th March. Dark threatening clouds this morning and rolling breakers sweeping up the beach. The gulls, screaming and calling, glided motionless on the strong winds off the sea. But the wild weather passed leaving an overcast sky and rain.

28th March. Cold North winds howling in the porch, rattling the door as it blusters around. The sea only just turns on the shore as ripples are blown away from the beach and large areas of water are swept backwards in eerie dark shadows.

30th March. The wild, blustery winds of the last few days finally blew themselves
out this morning. Occasionally the warm Spring sunshine broke through the clouds
only moments later to disappear again leaving the grey mistiness of threatening
rain showers. We drove through the narrow lanes to Umborne and Shute to look for
wild Daffodils but except for a few small patches of greenery, everything appeared
so dead or bare I despaired of finding any. We came across a clump of pure white
Snowdrops growing amongst the shorn stumps of hedge, so fresh they could not
have been out for long. In a sheltered place between high banks with a stream
running at the side of the road, we found the golden stars of Celandines, beautiful
clusters of Primroses and the first Dandelions but nothing like the splendour of
Spring in past years *(see below)*. We saw two Magpies in a field with a number of
Crows circling overhead and stopped at a gate to watch some chickens running free
as they always used to do in farm-yards. The Willows and Alders glowed orange
and red as their bare twigs caught the sunlight. And then, at last, we found some

Daffodils pushing their way through the dried Bracken
and grass at the roadside. I picked only a few, to paint
as it is a shame to take
them from their natural
surroundings. There

Dandelions, Daisies, Lesser Celandines,
Wild Daffodils & Primroses *(see 30th March)*

were more in a field and others tucked away in the hedge banks. It has been a lovely, mild day – just a little more sunshine and everything will begin to flourish.

31st March. Now that the strong North winds have dropped, the sea is again breaking on the shore and I lay in bed early this morning listening to the gentle sound of the waves. It has been a quiet, mild day with just a few spots of rain. Occasionally small areas of the cliff shone golden against the grey landscape but it was impossible to see where the sun had broken through the low cloud. Three or four huge pinnacles of rock could be clearly seen to be jutting out into the sea from what would normally appear to be the straight stretch of cliffs to Beer Head.

Lichens, Bracket Fungi and Moss on a rotting twig found at Rousdon

Lichens and Mosses found on our roof and stonework

Gentle showers on banks of Primrose,
Leaves unfolding fresh and green,
Rabbits scamper from their burrows,
Nests are hidden away, unseen.

Margaret I. Pogson

Cottage at Otterton *(see 5th April)*

APRIL

SILVER MOON

1st April. March went out like a lamb and April was heralded with a bright, mild, sunny morning – too bright, too early in fact as that often signifies rain and this was no exception. Sunshine and showers for the rest of the day and a clear starlit night with a sliver of silver moon.

3rd April. A very sharp frost this morning followed by a day promising sunshine but never quite getting round to it. Went for a short walk by the Coly and the wind was very cold. Found the first Daisies and Coltsfoot *(see below)* of the year. The Willow buds were just coming out and the Alders one mass of long graceful Catkins *(see page 51)* tinged with dark red. Some of the trees and bushes along the banks had dead foliage and driftwood entangled in their branches, so the flooding must have been quite severe at times during the Winter. During the afternoon there was a shower of hail and elsewhere, quite heavy snow-falls, but at last the buds are beginning to burst and lots of new green foliage is thrusting itself up from the cold Winter earth. We went on to Uplyme and returning later, through Rousdon, found the Pussy Willow *(see page 51)* was out. A Heron, poised with neck outstretched at a most ungainly angle, was busy fishing along Waterside.

Coltsfoot
(see 3rd April)

SPRING IS WITH US

4th April. Another frost early this morning but at last, the first real day of Spring with bright warm sunshine and a mildness in the air. I could feel the warmth on my back as I walked along the Old Beer Road, the birds singing and whistling in the trees and all the buds swelling and beginning to burst. A feeling of life everywhere, a surging forward, a lifting of the spirit, that unaccountable magic of Spring is with us. Whatever the weather from now on, at least Winter is behind us.

5th April. There was a frost early this morning and the misty blue-grey of Haven Cliff blended into a pale peach coloured sky. On our way to Exmouth the sun occasionally broke through the clouds lighting up distant patches of landscape and by the time we reached the estuary the far shore and sandbanks were golden in the morning light. The tide was in and the water so quiet and still the ripples barely turned on the smooth sandy beach. In the distance the hills of Dartmoor were pale and misty. On our way home we turned off the main road to go to Otterton and passed a tractor ploughing in a field. We could barely see it for a great flock of gulls circling above and settling around it. When we returned a few hours later the tractor was still ploughing but all the gulls had adjourned to a grassy field opposite and were standing in a circle: a most peculiar sight. We had stopped at Otterton to paint the cottages *(see page 48)*. It is a charming village with a series of tiny waterfalls, little bridges and fords where the paths to the houses cross a brook that runs at the side of the main street. The sky remained overcast with grey and hazy pink clouds and there were showers of rain and the sun breaking through with shafts of golden light.

Chantry Bridge *(see 10th April)*

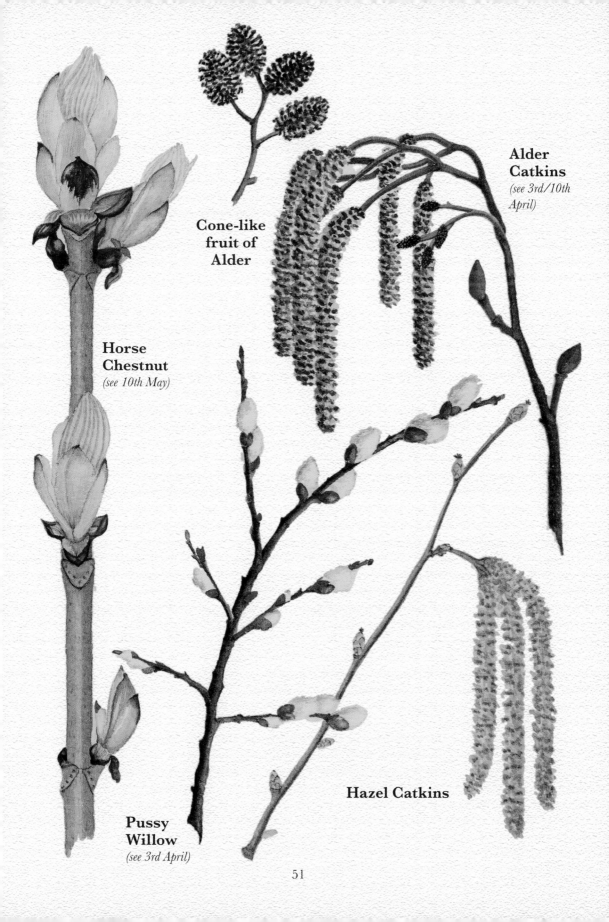

Horse Chestnut
(see 10th May)

Cone-like fruit of Alder

Alder Catkins
(see 3rd/10th April)

Pussy Willow
(see 3rd April)

Hazel Catkins

6th April. White Cliff and Beer Head were pale and misty this morning, with a gleam of silver light on the sea at the foot of the cliffs.

8th April. A very stormy night with hail and thunder and lightning from just before midnight until about 4 a.m. The morning dawned quiet and still with Haven Cliff grey against a metallic white reflection of sunlight on the distant sea. After the heavy rain last night, the marshes are flooded again. The evening tide was high and the Axe wide and still, reflecting the deep blue-grey clouds and peach pink of the evening sky.

10th April. We have had two days of heavy rain and the floods are rising on the marshes and the rivers running high. We went to the Mill Fields by the Coly this morning to pick more Alder Catkins *(see page 51)*. It didn't occur to us that they might be flooded but we were not surprised to find the usually quiet little river a raging torrent. The current swirling under Chantry Bridge, roaring over the rocks in a churning mass of dirty brown water *(see page 50)*. We could only get as far as the stile as the hollow was flooded. The river was well over the banks, sweeping through the trees and lapping over the grassy field. Pieces of driftwood and plants were swirling by and some bushes caught in the current, looked as though they would be swept away at any moment. I found some White Violets *(see below)* and the Goat Willow beginning to sprout. It was very mild with drizzle in the air that turned to torrential rain so we had to run for shelter.

Sweet Violet (White) *(see 10th April)*   **Woodland Violet**
                                               (see 29th April)   **Dog Violet**
                                                                     (see 29th April)

Sweet Violet
(see 29th April)

Ground Ivy
(see 19th May)

**Lesser
Periwinkle**
(see 27th April)

**Marsh
Marigolds**
(see 21st April)

**Wood
Anemones**
(see 21st April)

On the Slipway *(see 15th April)*

11th April. The roar of the sea woke me a number of time during the night. At 4.45 a.m. the tide seemed particularly high with great rollers sweeping in ominously in long straight lines. We feared the sea may be over again but it only swept shingle on to the pavement in one place. We went back to the Coly this morning to take some photographs of the flooded river but the water had already subsided and was cascading over the rocks, green and foaming.

WHITE HORSES

12th April. Despite the sunshine, it has been a cold, wild, windy day with white horses sweeping in on deep blue-green seas. The huge waves seemed to pause in mid-air before their crests curled over to crash on the beach in a mass of white spume and spray.

13th April. A very warm day with just the hint of a breeze. There was a beautiful golden atmosphere this evening as the sun set against a peach pink sky that shaded to a misty mauve and grey which looked very stormy. As the waves broke on the beach they caught the pink and golden light.

14th April. Today it was just like Summer with warm sunshine and balmy air from early morning as the sun slowly filtered through the mist and the clouds cleared to the still haze of evening. The sea was rolling with long straight waves and tumbling white crests of surf.

The Lagoon *(see 18th April)*

Devon Patchwork from Trow Hill *(see 26th April)*

BOAT-YARD VISIT

15th April. Before breakfast I went for a walk along the sea-front. The sea was silver and Haven Cliff the misty blue of a Summer's morning. Later, I went down to the boat-yard to paint as I knew the fishermen would be working on their boats ready for the coming season *(see page 54)*. Fortunately, I nearly completed my picture as when I returned in the afternoon, to put in the final touches, the boat had gone and the tide had ebbed, leaving mud-flats where there had been the wide expanse of water. During the evening I went down to the beach to help with a new Seine net that Bimbo Turner had made. They were trying it out to see if it was set correctly and hung well in the water. When we hauled it in we found we had caught a little green sand eel about 3ins. long. We experienced an odd illusion. As evening fell there appeared to be a mist over the surface of the sea but with a clear-cut edge in a semi-circle from the beach. Eventually we realised it was where the surface of the water was broke by the evening breeze compared the mirror-like stillness near the shore. But we couldn't account for the semi-circular shape. It has been a soft, warm day of gentle breezes and still water.

16th April. At 6.45 p.m. I helped Brian launch his boat and rowed as he shut his net. It was a beautiful evening, the sea was like a mill-pond. The gentle ripples on the surface slopped against the side of the boat and I could hear the quiet swish of the water on the pebbles. As the sun went down behind the cliffs, a blue mistiness settled over the surface of the sea.

18th April. The sunny days continue but the breezes are cold. Everywhere the birds are singing and gardens are bright with Spring flowers and fresh young leaves. I walked to the mouth of the river Axe to finish my painting of the estuary. To the East the sea has thrown up a high bank of shingle and carved out behind it a small lagoon *(see page 55)*.

19th April. A break in the weather. When I drew the kitchen curtains this morning, there was a heavy mist hanging over the marshes. The day remained cloudy with light rain in the evening.

Blackthorn and Buff-tailed Bumble Bee *(see 27th April)*

Farmyard at Combpyne

20th April. The cliffs were golden in the early morning sunlight and the crests of the waves brilliant against the blueness of the sea. The sun cast long shadows across the beach but it soon clouded over and turned cold in the wind.

GOLDEN SUNLIGHT

21st April. This evening I went to look for Marsh Marigolds *(see page 53)* in the boggy hollow near Cannington viaduct *(see page 162)*. It is always so squelchy I wore my wellingtons to avoid getting my feet wet. The lovely golden flowers were just coming out and had obviously not been affected by the late Spring. The Wood Anemones *(see page 53)* were carpeting the coppice with their delicate pink and white flowers and I found the first Bluebell of the season. All the buds on the trees were bursting, unfolding their crinkly leaves into the mildness of Spring. Celandines and Primroses covered the banks and the grass was dotted with the odd-looking spikes of Horsetails. They give me an odd creepy feeling as I always find them somewhat sinister and, indeed, they are poisonous to livestock. Alas the Greater Periwinkle by the bridge at Venlake appears to have suffered irretrievably from the harsh Winter. The long straight stems are threaded through the hedgerow but are still quite dead without any sign of growth. It was a beautiful, mild evening of gentle golden sunlight settling over the countryside, long shadows against the faint mist and a clear sky twinkling with stars. As we made our way home at about 9 p.m. it was still quite light with the sky in the West shading from pink to a deep subtle orange.

24th April. The clouds were beautiful today, moving across the sky in ever changing formations, dark and threatening, brilliant and majestic. There was a very heavy rainstorm and hail in the early afternoon followed by bright sunshine and showers.

26th April. Went to Exeter this morning and the view from Trow Hill was superb *(see page 56)*. All the hills and valleys were a patchwork of emerald green fields and red Devon soil sewn together with tidy straight hedges and dotted with farmsteads and little white cottages. Patches of blue sky showed between the clouds, the sun shining down to pick out some distant part of the landscape and make it brilliant with colour and light.

Water
Crowfoot

Herb
Robert
(see 9th May)

Giant
Horsetail

Alexanders

Wild Strawberry

Small White Butterfly

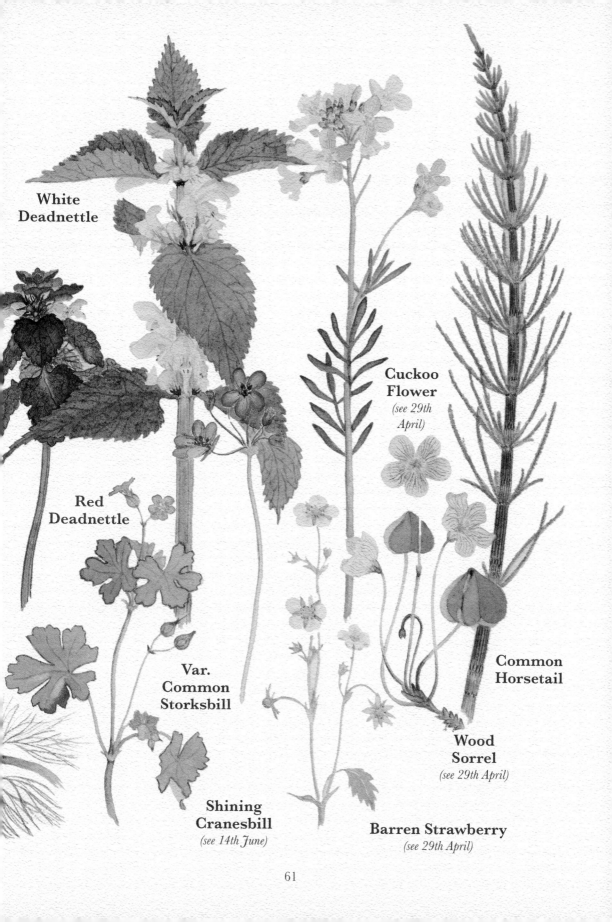

White
Deadnettle

Red
Deadnettle

Cuckoo
Flower
*(see 29th
April)*

Common
Horsetail

Var.
Common
Storksbill

Wood
Sorrel
(see 29th April)

Shining
Cranesbill
(see 14th June)

Barren Strawberry
(see 29th April)

PINK SKY

27th April. The evening was mild and still with a few thin dark clouds etched against a clear pink sky. The hills towards Shute faded into the marshes in a beautiful muted shade of blue with the silver waters of the Axe at high tide curving through the valley. The cloudy white blossoms of Blackthorn *(see page 57)* and blue of the Lesser Periwinkle *(see page 53)* along Waterside were just visible in the dim evening light.

28th April. There was a goose swimming on the sea this morning. We first noticed it at about 8.30 a.m. and later I heard it calling. I went to feed it and it was very hungry and exhausted and appeared to be quite old. The next time I looked, it had gone but it returned for a short while in the afternoon. Despite the sunshine it was quite cool today. A strong Northerly wind kept the sea calm, blowing the water away from shore so that it just rippled on the pebbles.

29th April. I picked Wood Sorrel *(see page 61)*, three different species of Violets *(see page 52)*, Barren Strawberry *(see page 61)* and Cuckoo flowers *(see page 61)* this morning, from the hedgerows and chalky fields around the Viaduct, The Ramsons are nearly out. I would have liked to have spent much longer searching for flowers along the lanes but I had to return home for lunch. We saw a Magpie again in a tree just above Shapwick Farm and there was a Blue Tit hopping about in the hedge.

30th April. The sunshine was lovely today but the wind cold. This evening, soft cream and warm grey clouds hung motionless in a pale sky and later there was gentle rain.

Evening

May

Cuckoos call across the meadows,
Soft pink petals drift from trees,
Bluebells carpet woodland shadows,
Hear the busy buzz of bees!

Margaret I. Pogson

Bluebells in Holyford Coppice

MAY

1st May. It was such a cold, wet, windy day it was more like Winter than May Day. Despite the weather we went to Umborne again to look for flowers in the hedgerows. The Primroses were lovely, great clusters of them clinging to the bank sides and the little blue Germander Speedwell *(see page 66)* with Violets, white Stitchwort and the brilliant colour of two Early Purple Orchids. The Cowslips are out at the top of the bank near Boshill Cross and the first white lacy flowers of Cow Parsley *(see page 66)* and masses of Blackthorn *(see page 168)*. When we returned, the Estuary was beautiful, all the silver and greys of reflected skies and wet mud.

SNOW IN MAY

2nd May. It snowed last night at Colyton and settled on the roofs of the houses like thick frost. A very cold and windy day with frequent heavy rain, sleet and snow storms. During the morning snow was blowing across the marshes in dense clouds but it did not settle. Between the storms the sun broke through the clouds, warm and brilliant against a blue sky. There was a most spectacular cloud over the sea this evening. It was like a plateau with tall curved sides and appeared to have a castle on the summit, all pink and cream in the sunset like something from a fairy tale.

Apple Blossom

Ladybird

**Cow
Parsley**
(see 1st May)

**Persian
Speedwell**

**Yellow
Rocket**

**Germander
Speedwell**
(see 1st May)

4th May. It has been a still, mild day with much sunshine, a great improvement after all the recent rough, cold weather. The evening was calm and peaceful with the sea turquoise and silver. Golden light radiated from the stark edge of a dark cloud in the West against a backcloth of muted pink and mauve-grey clouds. Late evening was clear and cold, hung with stars and a crescent moon with a hint of frost.

6th May. For the last two nights we have had 4°F of frost.

10th May. After days of milder weather, sunshine and showers, it has turned colder again. It was very wet all day and became stormy in the evening with rough seas, white horses and dense rain mists. The hedgerows are now quite green with fresh young leaves and the roadsides are scattered with late Spring flowers. The Horse Chestnuts *(see page 51)* are in full leaf on Trow Hill and the banks are gloriously dotted with Primroses but the Bluebells *(see page 78)* are still reluctant to appear.

11th May. Today it suddenly turned much warmer and very humid.

12th May. I first awoke at 5.30 a.m. to all the sounds of Summer, the sea breaking on the beach and the early morning cry of the gulls, I was soon lulled back to sleep and when I finally got up, it was to a still, mild morning not quite knowing whether to promise sunshine or rain. It was mid-afternoon before the sun broke through and it became very humid. While I was hanging out the washing this morning, Mr Seagull flew over to the porch roof and stood there watching me. I spoke to him, as usual, and he answered with quiet little noises like the quacking of a duck. Mrs Seagull appears to be nesting again but after last year's futile efforts I suppose there is little

Nesting between the Chimney-pots *(see 12th May)*

Combpyne *(see 10th June)*

likelihood of a family. I haven't seen their funny courting antics this year. They are usually such proud, severe birds, it is hilarious to see them become so preoccupied and absent minded. They wander around the middle of the road, Mr Seagull trailing long pieces of nesting material until he eventually presents them to his mate. The babies look very odd, all fluffy and spotted and it is hard to believe they will mature into such elegant birds *(see pages 37 and 67)*.

13th May. The countryside has come alive during the past week. Hedgerows are thick with greenery, the Bluebells are beginning to spread their beautiful carpets in ribbons along the roadsides and the trees and bushes are laden with blossom. I picked some Stitchwort, Celandines, Bluebells and Blackthorn and found another early Purple Orchid on Boshill. I haven't heard the Cuckoo yet but have been told they are about. Mist and low cloud hung around all day and turned to heavy drizzle in the evening.

GLORIOUS DAY

14th May. A very heavy mist this morning and it was sometime before it cleared from the sea. Even then it hung over the Axe in a dense cloud but gradually thinned out up stream. It soon became apparent it was going to be a glorious day and when the sun came out it was hot with wispy Mare's Tails spread across the sky and a light breeze to keep it pleasant. As evening settled, the sea rolled in, sometimes breaking over the ridge in a succession of larger waves and then becoming still again.

The sky faded from blue to blend with the pink and mauve of the horizon and the cliffs became pale and misty in the evening light. Above the sound of the sea, I could hear a Blackbird singing in the trees at the Grove, a lovely melody to end a perfect day.

Stormy Weather

15th May. Very hazy with the cliffs barely visible in the heat of the day, just soft blue images across the still water. The sunset a fiery red ball which should promise another day of good weather although it seemed somewhat cooler this evening.

FIRST SWALLOW

16th May. There was a change in the weather this morning. It was dull and cool and yet the birds were singing merrily and I saw the first Swallow. The sea was dark and sombre and as grey clouds gathered, the wind freshened to gale force bringing rain in the evening. The waves became stormy, topped with white horses and rolled onto the beach in a confusion of noise and flying spray.

17th May. The wild windy weather continued today with long sweeping waves rolling in from the S.W. It was exhilarating to watch the wildness of the sea against the briefly sun lit cliffs and dark threatening clouds. The wind dropped but the sea continued to pound the beach with roaring waves and rain lashed the windows.

After the Storm

18th May. A much quieter day but rain in the evening with a beautiful sunset of shades of gold and pink blending with grey.

MY WELSH HOLIDAY

19th May. I started my holiday today and travelled by train to join a painting party at Llansantffraid. It was a lovely journey as the countryside was fresh and green and the railway banks were a glorious profusion of wild flowers. In places they were covered with Cowslips *(see page 78)* and there were many Bluebells and drifts of Stitchwort. I saw a heron fishing and another with its large wings outstretched in flight. I was surprised to see so many rabbits again, scampering along with their fluffy white tails a bobbing, frisky little lambs butting their mothers in play and some bullocks with rich brown and white thick curly coats. There was a field of shorn sheep and two fields of fat pink pigs. I saw a small copse, yellow with Marsh Marigolds and many more growing in clumps by ditches and streams. There was warmth and sunshine all the way. I was met at Gobowen Station and driven through the countryside to my hotel, Bryn Tanat Hall. It is a lovely spot, wild gardens running down to the river, beautiful trees and the birds whistling and singing well into the evening. There are wild flowers everywhere, Yellow Archangel *(see page 77)*, Ground Ivy *(see page 53)*, Violets, Cuckoo Flowers and the first Red Campion I have seen this year. I am sure it is going to be a lovely holiday.

20th May. I woke early and watched the changing light on the distant hills. They look quite blue in the evening and early morning and yet when the sun shines directly on to them, the trees and rocks with the monument at the top are very distinct. In the late afternoon I walked to Llanyblodwel to post some letters and was delighted to find so many Elms in the hedges with great clusters of seeds forming. The Dutch Elm disease has just about killed them all in the Axe valley and yet here they are still growing in profusion. The Hazel flowers have set and the nuts are beginning to form. I found some Ramsons *(see page 78)* by the river, a Lords and Ladies *(see page 79)* and the cone of a Norway Spruce *(see page 80)*.

21st May. We spent the day painting at Llanyblodwel, sitting by the bridge over the Tanat. It was very peaceful with the sound of the water running over the stones and the doves cooing in the trees. I heard a Woodpecker and a Cuckoo and the cawing of Rooks and Crows, all the sweet music of Summer drifting across the countryside.

The River Lym

22nd May. Went for a walk by the river before breakfast. The morning was fresh and clear and the woods smelled of damp air and foliage. I had to pick my way carefully as the path was very slippery in places with steep muddy banks and rough stones. I found some Alternate-leaved Golden Saxifrage *(see page 78)* and the new young growth of Spruce like spiky green caterpillars. We went to Oswestry in the afternoon and on our way back the clouds were beautiful, great masses of them billowing across the sky all creamy white and every shade of blue and grey.

24th May. I woke sometime during the quiet stillness of the night and could hear the owls in the garden. The usual hooting was probably a Tawny Owl and then there was the dreadful screech of a Barn Owl. The dawn was beautiful, pale mauve-grey clouds against a blue-green sky. I lay in bed at 5.30 a.m. with the curtains drawn back looking at the view and listening to the dawn chorus. All manner of birds were singing and yet by listening carefully you could hear each individual song. In the late afternoon dark thundery clouds silhouetted the quarry buildings and towering formations gathered in the sky. The brilliant colour of a pink and mauve sunset tinted the whole of the surrounding landscape.

BACK TO DEVON

26th May. I went for a short walk before breakfast to collect some Elm seeds to paint and then prepared to leave for home. It was a dismal journey with rain all the way and it must have been very wet in Devon during the past few days, as the rivers and streams were swiftly flowing torrents of dirty brown water. I saw a young bullock chasing two muddy pink piglets that had obviously been annoying him. Despite the weather, the English countryside was as beautiful as ever, the trees and hedgerows were fresh and green and the meadows bright with flowers. Here in Devon, the Bluebells are out all along the roadsides but I didn't see any like that where I was staying in Wales. I enjoyed my holiday very much and hope one day to return to Bryn Tanat Hall.

Spruce

27th May. It has been a day of brilliant sunshine but the cold wind freshened and the sea became wild.

28th May. It turned very cold today and was wild and stormy with much rain. By evening huge breakers were lashing the shore and we wondered if the sea would be over again. It is such foul weather for May, the worst I have ever known for the month.

STOURHEAD

29th May. After all the unreliable weather lately, the morning gradually brightened and glorious sunshine filled the sky as we went Stourhead. The Crab Apple *(see page 142)* blossom was out in the hedgerows and Cow Parsley, Garlic Mustard *(see page 79)*, Wild Mustard, Charlock *(see page 77)* and Bugle *(see page 79)* were growing profusely along the roadsides. It was a lovely warm day with the blue sky full of fluffy white clouds. The Rhododendrons and Azaleas were out and the trees magnificent with their contrasting foliage and finely patterned bark. On the lake there were ducks and ducklings, Moorhens with their chicks and a most disagreeable Swan. Some ducklings had to swim for cover under some overhanging trees while their mother bravely lured the Swan away from them. He stretched his neck and beat his wings nearly standing on the water before swimming away. The day ended with a most beautiful red sunset.

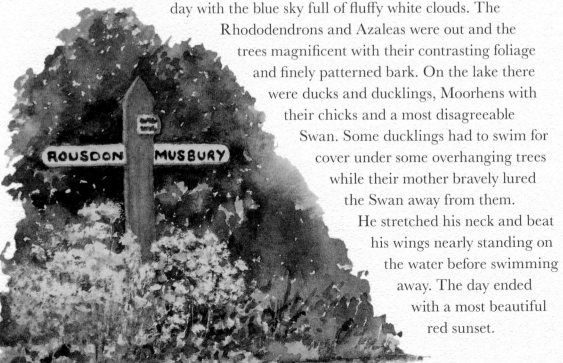

ROUSDON   MUSBURY

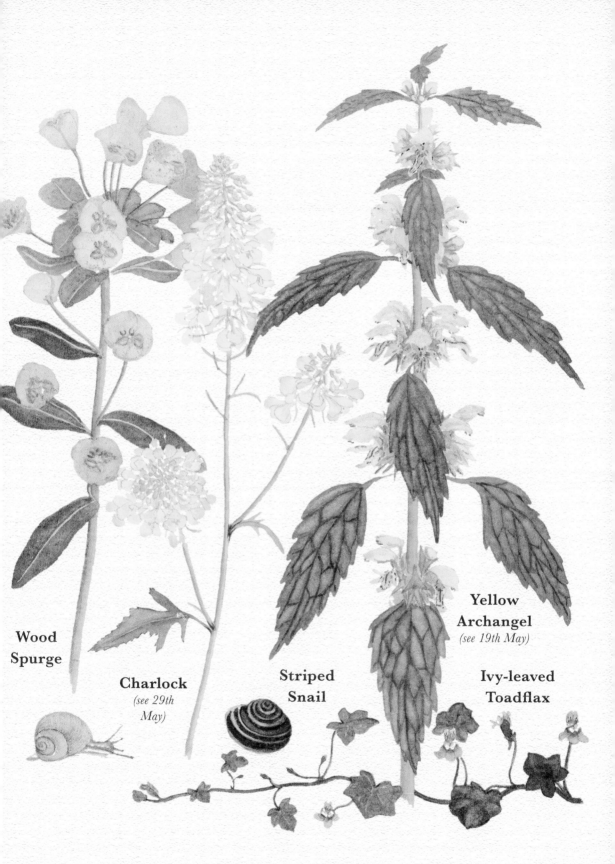

Wood Spurge

Charlock
(see 29th May)

Striped Snail

Yellow Archangel
(see 19th May)

Ivy-leaved Toadflax

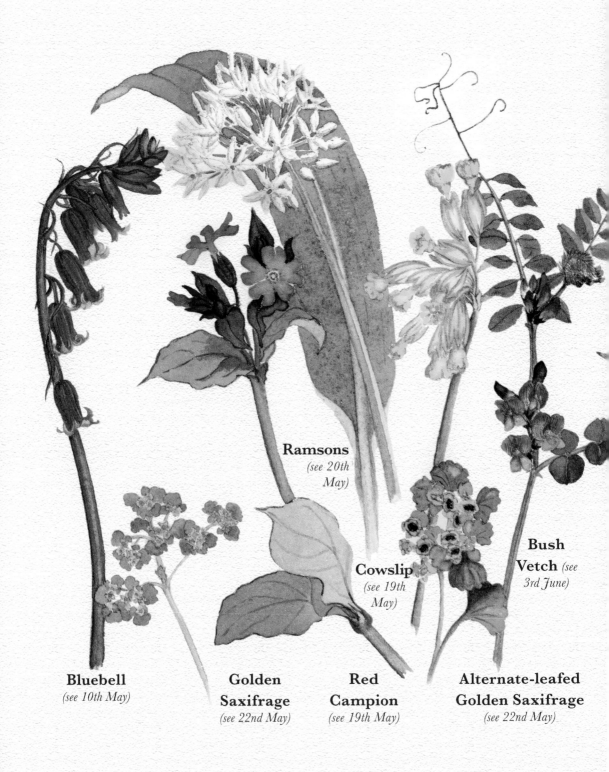

Ramsons
(see 20th May)

Cowslip
(see 19th May)

Bush Vetch *(see 3rd June)*

Bluebell
(see 10th May)

Golden Saxifrage
(see 22nd May)

Red Campion
(see 19th May)

Alternate-leafed Golden Saxifrage
(see 22nd May)

arlic
tard
*(29th
May)*

Early
Purple
Orchid
(see 13th May)

Lord &
Ladies
*(see 13th
May)*

Wild
Turnip

Greater
Periwinkle
(see 7th June)

Bugle
(see 29th May)

Bird's-foot
Trefoil

Greater
Stitchwood

Larch Cones

30th May. Prolonged and heavy rain throughout the day caused severe flooding at Charmouth. Holiday caravans were washed away as thunder storms and drenching downpours continued. It lessened towards late afternoon and the evening was calm and still with the sea bright red and grey with flood water and dotted with bright red sails. Another spectacular sunset filled the sky.

31st May. By mid-morning the sun had broken through the mist and became a lovely warm day. The flooding is still serious in Dorset but at last the rain has stopped. A mild gentle evening, the air was quite still and the muted colours of the sky shading from blue and mauve to grey and peach on the horizon.

Cones: Norway Spruce, Pine and Douglas Fir
(see 20th May)

June

All the heady scents of Summer,
Elderflowers and new-mown hay,
Sparkling light on distant water,
Long, still evenings end the day.

Margaret I. Pogson

Devon Lane

JUNE

SUMMER ARRIVES

1st June. Summer is here at last however briefly it remains. Golden sunshine and blue sky from early morning brought the warmth and stillness of a perfect Summer's day. There was a beautiful pink and blue sunset with a hazy mist settling over the sea and the gentle sound of ripples on the beach.

3rd June. The day was very still and overcast and quite cool at times. Towards evening the sea was like a mirror and silent beneath a heavy mist. The hedgerows along the road to Rousdon and Ware Cross are a picture. This morning I picked some of my favourite flowers from the banks of lacy Cow Parsley and Bluebells, the brilliant patches of Campion and white dustings of Stitchwort. There are Buttercups and Vetch *(see page 79)*, the flowers of the Wayfaring Tree, Daisies and Plantain, Clover, Speedwell and Herb Robert *(see page 60)*, the first flowers of Alkanet *(see page 87)* at Axmouth and, at last the May blossom.

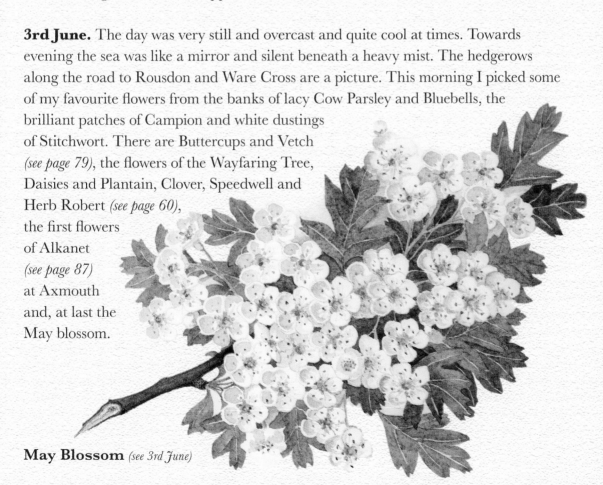

May Blossom *(see 3rd June)*

THE BEAUTY OF DEVON HEDGEROWS

It would be difficult to surpass the beauty of the Devon hedgerows in May and June. I have a great love and admiration of wild plants and flowers. They do not have the coddled existence of the well-kept garden but a constant struggle against adversity, greenfly, ants, slugs and snails, floods and drought, exhaust fumes and the disastrous hedge and roadside trimmers. Year after year they reappear in all their splendour, competing with each other for space and yet existing in joyous harmony.

5th June. I went to Hillhead today and sat in the sheltered corner of a field to paint a stile and surrounding plants. It was a beautiful day, the birds were singing and the sun was hot on my back. From the top of the hill, the wide expanse of rolling countryside spread out before me, a magnificent view from Colcombe, the Umborne Valley and Shute Hill to Axminster, Trinity Hill and Musbury Castle. Boshill and Stedcombe House were clearly visible with the Axe winding its way along the valley to the sea passed Hawkesdown and Haven Cliff.

Stile at Colyton					**Letter-box at Boshill Cross**

Wood
Avens
(see 14th June)

Yellow
Pimpernel
(see 10th June)

Fragrant
Orchid

Comfrey
(see 14th June)

Tormentil
(see 14th June)

Small
Tortoiseshell
Butterfly

Ragged
Robin
(see 10th June)

Bistort
(see 10th June)

Red
Admiral
Butterfly

Honeysuckle and Wild Roses *(see 13th July)*

Meadow Brown Butterfly   **Speckled Wood Butterfly**

Alkanet
(see 3rd July)

Elder
(see 8th July)

**Bladder
Campion**

**Streaked
Cranesbill**

White Campion

Foxglove
(see 16th/24th June)

Musbury Church *(see 19th June)*

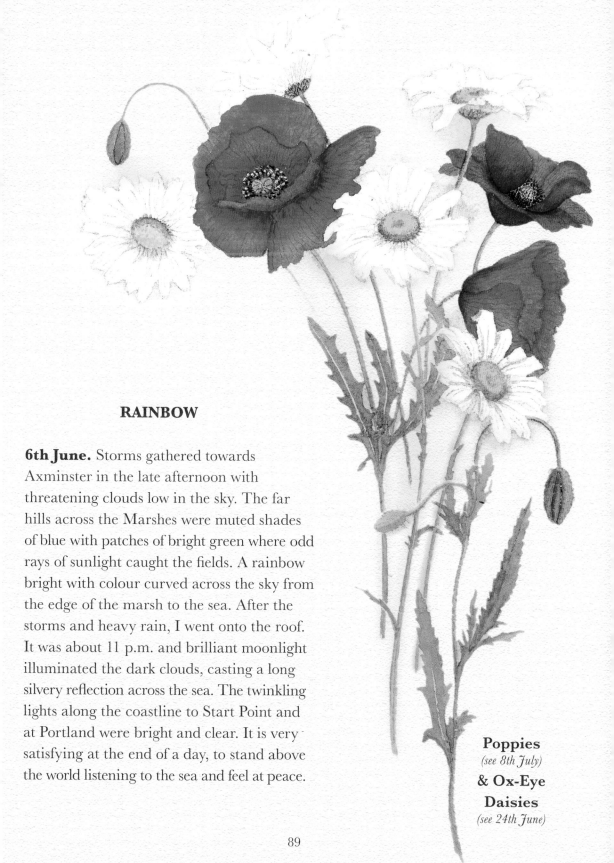

RAINBOW

6th June. Storms gathered towards
Axminster in the late afternoon with
threatening clouds low in the sky. The far
hills across the Marshes were muted shades
of blue with patches of bright green where odd
rays of sunlight caught the fields. A rainbow
bright with colour curved across the sky from
the edge of the marsh to the sea. After the
storms and heavy rain, I went onto the roof.
It was about 11 p.m. and brilliant moonlight
illuminated the dark clouds, casting a long
silvery reflection across the sea. The twinkling
lights along the coastline to Start Point and
at Portland were bright and clear. It is very
satisfying at the end of a day, to stand above
the world listening to the sea and feel at peace.

Poppies
(see 8th July)
**& Ox-Eye
Daisies**
(see 24th June)

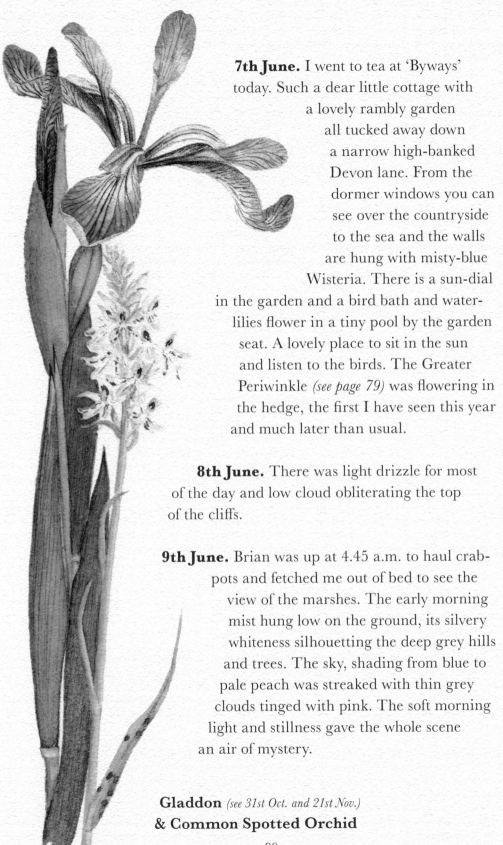

7th June. I went to tea at 'Byways' today. Such a dear little cottage with a lovely rambly garden all tucked away down a narrow high-banked Devon lane. From the dormer windows you can see over the countryside to the sea and the walls are hung with misty-blue Wisteria. There is a sun-dial in the garden and a bird bath and water-lilies flower in a tiny pool by the garden seat. A lovely place to sit in the sun and listen to the birds. The Greater Periwinkle *(see page 79)* was flowering in the hedge, the first I have seen this year and much later than usual.

8th June. There was light drizzle for most of the day and low cloud obliterating the top of the cliffs.

9th June. Brian was up at 4.45 a.m. to haul crab-pots and fetched me out of bed to see the view of the marshes. The early morning mist hung low on the ground, its silvery whiteness silhouetting the deep grey hills and trees. The sky, shading from blue to pale peach was streaked with thin grey clouds tinged with pink. The soft morning light and stillness gave the whole scene an air of mystery.

Gladdon *(see 31st Oct. and 21st Nov.)*
& Common Spotted Orchid

10th June. This morning we went to Uplyme and returned via Venlake and under the viaduct to Shapwick. I found the first Ragged Robin *(see page 85)* I have seen for years in the hollow where the Marsh Marigolds grow. A pretty blue butterfly flitted amongst the grass on a bank nearby where Bugle, Sorrel and Yellow Pimpernel *(see page 85)* were growing. The sheep on the grassy slopes around the farm had recently been sheared and looked like the wooden toys from a Noah's Ark. At Combpyne I found a plant I have not seen before which later I identified as Bistort *(see page 85)*. There was a Heron fishing in the Axe so close to the road we had a really good view of him wading along with his neck outstretched ready to strike.

12th June. How variable the weather is! After a glorious sunny day yesterday it has now turned damp and dull with low cloud over the cliffs and rain by early evening.

BREATH-TAKING VIEW

14th June. We were at Uplyme again this afternoon and came home by Cathole and Woodhouse Hill crossing to Musbury by the back lanes. There was still many Bluebells in the woods at Cathole and the new ferns were enormous, some of them 2-3 feet long. I found pink and white Clover *(see page 97)*, Comfrey *(see page 85)*, Wood Avens *(see page 85)*, Tormentil *(see page 85)* and numerous grasses. On the far side of a hedge I could just see the top of a bright yellow shrub which looked very much like Broom but I hadn't time to investigate. The view at the top of the hill before descending to Musbury, was breath-taking. The rich patchwork of fields and undulating countryside was spread out against a backcloth of distant-hills and the river winding its way along the valley. We could see the roads to Axminster and Whitford and the bridge. We have had so much rain the Yellow Flags *(see page 96)* growing in the ditch along the Musbury Road were standing in water. I find it very difficult to list all the flowers I see as there are so many new ones each week at this time of year. This morning I found the tiny pink Shining Cranesbill *(see page 61)* on the bank opposite Auntie Eva's house. We saw two Magpies in the lane and along Waterside a Cormorant stood drying its wings.

Early Morning Mist on Seaton Marshes

15th June. Another variable day with cold blustery winds more appropriate to March and the short, sharp showers of April but the sea was a beautiful deep blue and there were frequent sunny spells. Although the sunset was quite ordinary, the whole 360⁰ of the horizon was a lovely dusky pink shading to mauve and blue, later turning to red.

HEAVEN'S GATE

16th June. This evening I walked up the track to Heaven's Gate with Brian. Despite all the rain we have had recently, it was dry most of the way. The view from the top over Lyme Bay to Golden Cap was beautiful in the mellow evening sunlight. The grasses were high in the meadow and dotted with Buttercups, Daisies and the little Self-Heal *(see page 96)*. We followed the path back through the woods and heard a continuous creaking noise which we finally decided was coming from two trees rubbing together in the breeze. The Foxgloves *(see page 87)* were in full bud but it will be a few more days before the Wild Roses are out. As we made our way home the sun was setting a fiery red ball in a clear red sky. From Boshill the whole panoramic landscape was suffused with glowing colour and the waters of the Axe were pink.

Lobster
(see 17th June)

**Edible
Crab**
(see 17th June)

CRABBING

17th June. I was up at 5.30 to be ready to go crabbing at 6 a.m. The golden light of the early morning sun shining from a clear sky, cast long dark shadows across the beach. The tide was low so it took some time to launch the boat, one man working the winch and the other heaving with his back to the boat and placing the timbers on which it slides into the water. When the tide is high you can often climb on-board between the waves without even getting your feet wet but this morning I took off my shoes and socks and paddled out. I sat on the fore-cuddy as the pots were hauled, cleared and re-bated, the Seagulls wheeling overhead as they waited for scraps. One even hitched a ride on the mizzen mast. Owing to the low tide we had to leave three pots at the mouth of the Axe as they were fast on the rocks. We inched our way in to get close enough to free them but it became too shallow and rocky so it was decided we should collect them on our way back. We passed Finger and Thumb Rock and then Corban Rock where a Cormorant stood drying its outstretched wings. As we rounded Culverhole Point we could see the

Spiny Spider Crab
(see 17th June)

Yellow Flag
(see 14th June)

Self-Heal
(see 16th June)

Monkey Flower (Llants)

Hedge Woundwort
(see 22nd June)

Water Cress

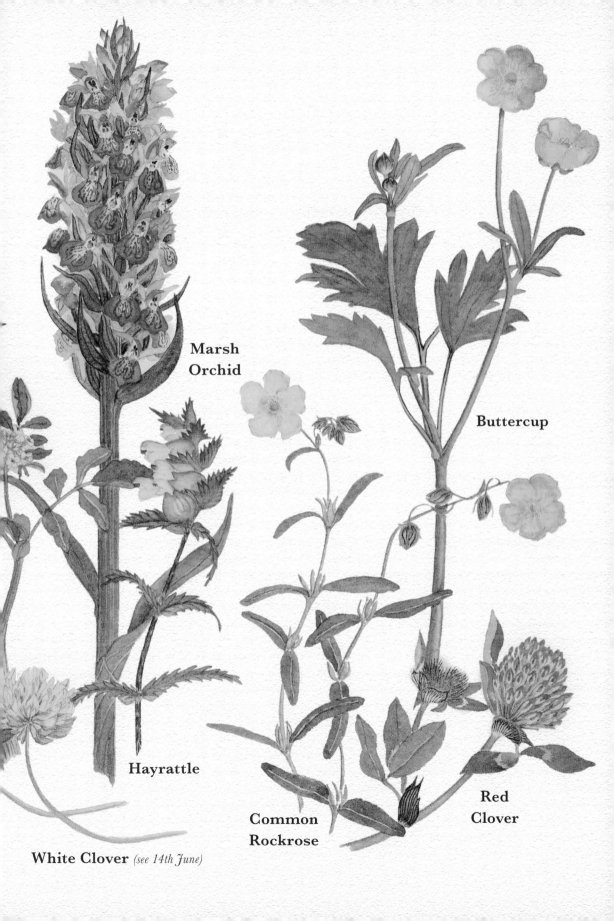

Marsh Orchid

Buttercup

Hayrattle

White Clover *(see 14th June)*

Common Rockrose

Red Clover

wreck of the *Fairway* which went aground on 2nd December 1978. The rusting hull minus its masts, looked desolate, abandoned high and dry on the rocks. The sky gradually clouded over, the sun barely penetrating the mist that settled. Golden Cap and Charmouth were grey silhouettes against a pale pink horizon, the water beneath them shimmering in the great shafts of light that shone down from behind the dark clouds. A lone bird flew its solitary course across the sea. The pots were hauled from 8 and 15 fathoms and we made for home with a catch of 5 Lobsters, 3 large Crabs and numerous Spider Crabs *(see pages 94/95)*. There was also a Blin which was found swimming around in one of the pots. We arrived back at 9.15 a.m. and I was carried ashore so that I didn't have to get wet wading in.

Ribwart Plantain, Great Plantain & Nottingham Catchfly

18th June. Mrs Seagull has two fluffy chicks. This morning I heard them squeaking as I was hanging out the washing and when I looked over to their nest they were tottering about amongst the chimney pots. A glorious day of clear blue skies and hot sunshine gradually fading to a still misty evening.

DROWSY SOUNDS OF SUMMER

19th June. Another glorious day, with the sea like a mirror and the cliffs distant in the pale morning haze. The fishing boats coming in with the morning catch cut steadily widening V's in the still water. I spent the day painting at Musbury and enjoyed the peace and tranquillity of the country churchyard *(see page 88)*. The church clock struck steadily on the hour and swallows nesting in the porch flew back and forth busily feeding their young. I could hear the distant drone of a motor mower and the snip of shears as someone trimmed around the graves. With the drowsy sounds of Summer in the heat of the day it was very difficult to concentrate on my work and I was thankful for the shade of a majestic Yew.

20th June. The early morning was warm and hazy but gradually a thick sea mist drifted in, obliterating the cliffs. It persisted throughout the day, blotting out the sun and leaving the atmosphere cold and damp.

21st June. There are three very active baby seagulls all squeaking for food. Their parents often come to the roof and nearly beg for the scraps I have for them.

22nd June. Went to Whitford Weir *(see page 34)* to see if I could find any water-plants but there were only the normal Rushes and Yellow Flags. The Silverweed *(see page 112)* and Hedge Woundwort *(see page 96)* were out and the rampant growth of Hogweed and Hemlock with its purple spotted stems. Just above the weir the water was deep and green with sinister eddies slowly moving around the rocks.

Early Morning at Sea

24th June. The Wild Roses and Foxgloves *(see pages 86/87)* are out in the hedgerows and I saw the first Poppy today. The Ox-Eye Daisies *(see page 89)* have been out for some time and look lovely dotted amongst the grass with Hawkbit on the banksides at Axmouth and Boshill Cross. On the way to Rousdon there is a field of Mustard, a great expanse of brilliant yellow.

ADDERS ABOUT!

29th June. The weather is very unsettled, sometimes cool, windy and overcast then sunny and hot but very little rain. There are many Adders about this year and specific warning of them at Seaton Hole where a dog was bitten by one recently.

30th June. From Boshill this evening we could see the twinkling lights of Colyton and Colyford in the valley below, against the deep blues and greens of the distant hills. As night enfolded the scene, thin lines of blue and pale yellow light shone from between the dark bands of steely-grey clouds that made up the sky.

Fairy Ring Toadstools

July

Long hot days of Summer sunshine,
Thunderstorms and drenching rain,
Scarlet poppies by the roadside,
Golden fields of ripening grain.

Margaret I. Pogson

Thatchers at work on Queen Street *(see 4th July)*

JULY

SEAWEED, CRABS AND WHELKS

1st July. I went out with the fishing boat at 6 a.m. this morning. The wind was cold but the clouds were broken and there was much light in the sky, promising a fine day. We could see the early morning sun shining on the red cliffs at Sidmouth but we had to wait for the clouds to clear before it came out at intervals, bright and warm. The Cormorants were drying their wings and the Salmon leaping as we went close inshore to haul some pots. I lay on the fore cubby and looked down into the clear green water to another world. Beautiful fronds of seaweed, all different shapes and colours like tropical plants undulated in the current. There were fire bright green threads, wide straps of burnt umber and dark green ribbons against glistening white rocks and patches of sand *(see pages 120/121)*.

After cleaning the pots we had about 14 Edible Crabs, some Whelks and endless quantities of Spiny Spider Crabs, but no Lobsters. I was given a Hermit Crab *(see page 120)* in a Whelk shell and took him home to paint. He ventured out onto the draining-board but when I approached he shot back into his shell with a sudden clicking noise. I fetched a bucket of sea water and when I put him in he left his home and crawled around the bottom. The soft pink sack-like shape of his body looked very unattractive and I wondered if I had done him some harm. However he soon

Hedge Bindweed

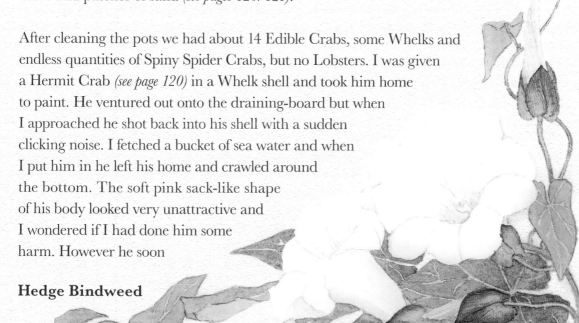

**Dame's
Violet**

**Large-flowered
Evening Primrose**
(see 20th Sept.)

**Spear
Thistle**
(see 29th July)

**Marsh
Woundwort**
(see 17th July)

**Yellow
Corydalis**

Common Mallow
(see 3rd July)

Hybrid Campion

Pyramid Orchid

Musk Mallow

Painted Lady Butterfly

Creeping Cinquefoil
(see 5th Aug.)

Track to the Sea *(see 10th July)*

made his way back inside his shell by clasping it with all his legs and easing it around until his body was just inside the opening. Then, with a sudden movement he was in and neatly tucked away. It really was quite incredible how he could fit so much of himself into so small a space. I watched, fascinated as he waved his small feeders in front of his mouth, a constant circulation of water moving around him. We are calling him Albert and after finishing my painting have left him to spend the night in some sea-water in a cool place. It has been a beautiful day, sunny and hot, but this evening it turned quite cold. The first quarter of the moon is shining brightly from a clear sky.

2nd July. Alas I found poor Albert dead this morning. How I wished I had returned him to the sea instead of keeping him overnight for my own selfish use. I feel so guilty at ending his life so unnecessarily and in future will not attempt to keep anything away from its natural surroundings.

3rd July. The gorgeous weather continues with hot sunny days and clear blue skies. The Common Mallow *(see page 107)* flowers are out and I found a massive plant of the lovely purple Tufted Vetch *(see page 113)* on Seaton Down Hill. As Evening closed in, the Swifts screamed around the flat and the air turned cold and damp. A heavy white mist settled over the marshes but the sky was clear and the moon shone over the sea.

4th July. The thatchers are working on a roof in Queen Street so I went to paint them today *(see page 104)*. I watched them lay the wheat-reed and trim it to achieve that lovely golden velvety finish of new thatch. It is a most impressive craft much to be admired.

Feverfew

Whitlands *(see 10th July)*

6th July. I finished my painting of the thatchers today and they told me about their work. When the weather is bad in Winter, they go to Slapton Sands to cut reeds but never gather enough to last them throughout the year. Some of the wheat-reed is grown near Sidmouth. I remember seeing it last year, in stooks in a field on the top road. Another glorious day ending with the sun a glowing, deep red ball in the sky.

7th July. Brilliant sunshine this morning but later the sky became overcast and it turned somewhat cooler.

8th July. Very little sunshine today but humid and at times it looked very stormy. The Honeysuckle is thick in the hedgerows, great masses of yellow and pink with Foxgloves and Tufted Vetch and the lovely cream Burnet Rose. The Elderflowers *(see page 87)* are a picture with the trails of pink wild Roses and the flat heads of tall Hogweed. The Ragwort *(see page 113)* is out on the corner by Axmouth Bridge and the brilliant scarlet Poppies *(see page 89)*. The wild flowers are very profuse this Summer and appear to be particularly robust. We saw a Yellowhammer in the lane by Ware Cross.

STARRY SKY

9th July. There was a sparrow fluttering at our bedroom window today and I thought perhaps there was a nest on the ledge but later realised it was catching insects as I saw it with a beak full of them. It is a beautiful night with just a few wispy clouds in a clear sky. A large round silver moon is trailing its reflection right across the sea from the horizon to the shore. There are twinkling lights everywhere from the stars in the sky, at Portland and along the coast to Start Point and from passing ships on the horizon.

The Main Gate

Knapweed

Tarrow

Milkwort

Silverweed
(see 22nd June)

**Field
Scabious**
(see 15th July))

Wood Sage
(see 29th July)

112

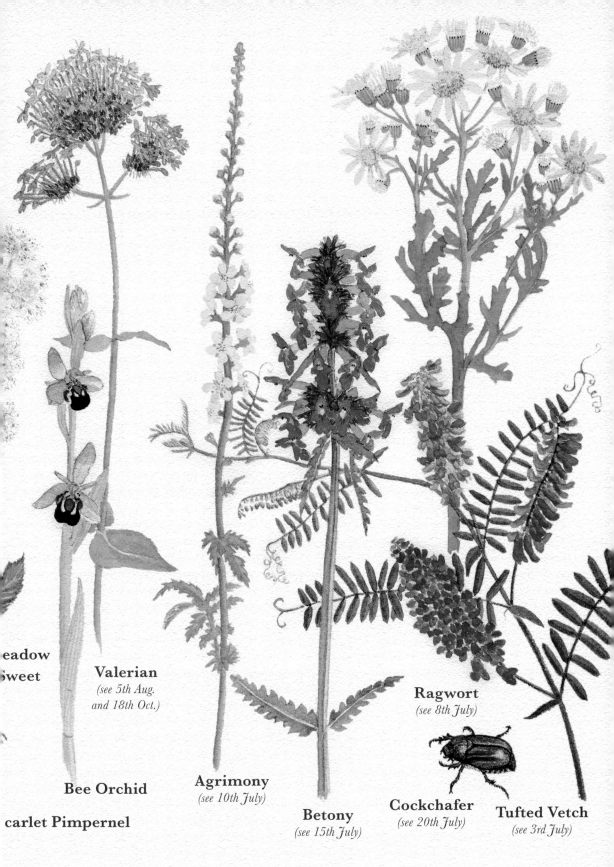

eadow
sweet

Valerian
*(see 5th Aug.
and 18th Oct.)*

Bee Orchid

carlet Pimpernel

Agrimony
(see 10th July)

Betony
(see 15th July)

Ragwort
(see 8th July)

Cockchafer
(see 20th July)

Tufted Vetch
(see 3rd July)

Seaton Marshes and the Axe Valley

10th July. We painted at Whitlands today *(see page 110)*. The Swallows are nesting under the eaves of the old house and were busy feeding their young. The Hogweed is rampant along the track to the sea *(see page 108)* and the Elders heavy with flowers. Yesterday I made the first Elderflower Champagne of the season. The Agrimony *(see page 113)* is out at Boshill Cross and the Meadowsweet laden with pollen. The tall spikes of Rose Bay Willow Herb are just coming into flower, always a sign that Summer is advancing. The sun was setting when we returned from Sidmouth and from the top of Trow Hill we could see it catching the roofs of the houses at Sidford. It bathed the country-side in mellow evening light which faded into a smoky blue in the distance. We came home by the Axe, the peachy-red sunset streaked across the sky, reflecting in the wide still water of high tide, all silvery-pink and steely-grey.

11th July. There was another very high tide this morning covering the mud-banks of the Axe. The boats in the harbour were bobbing about on their moorings, the rigging tinkling like the sound of tiny bells. Last night I saw another odd effect of the moonlight. The

moon was shining from behind a mottled pattern of dark clouds with a bank of low cloud preventing any reflection on the sea except for a golden glow far away on the horizon.

12th July. There was a most peaceful scene in the field above the harbour, this morning. A ram with large curled horns was grazing with the sheep, their woolly coats pale against the rich green grass and long dark shadows cast by the early morning sunlight. The river was choppy with little white horses right up to Axmouth as the strong current of the inflowing tide met the stiff North winds blowing down the valley.

13th July. The weather continues hot and humid although out of the sun the breeze feels cool. We are at the height of Summer, the hedgerows are entwined with fragrant pink and cream Honeysuckle and Wild Roses *(see page 86)* cascade everywhere. I have never seen the Elderflowers so profuse. The still air heady with the scent of their rich blossoms and the Bees dusted with so much pollen. The large spikes of Foxglove vie with the early flowering Rose Bay Willow Herb and tangles of blue and purple Tufted Vetch. The birds finish nesting and the fledglings stretch their wings and flutter away. Butterflies flit from flower to flower and a great stillness over the countryside in the heat of the day. Cows stand idly wafting their tails to flick away the flies as other creatures slip away to seek shade from the mid-day sun. In the coolness of the evening Swifts scream around the eaves and as the sun settles behind the hills, the soft scents of Summer linger in the air. The Grasshoppers chirrup as the light fades from the sky and another fine Summer's day comes to an end.

15th July. This morning Mr. Seagull took two Mackerel from me as I held them. If I persisted in feeding them by hand I think they would become quite tame. It was a most beautiful morning. I awoke to the gentle sound of the sea and a misty stillness blending from sky to shore with barely any indication of the horizon. At high tide the Axe was quite still, without any noticeable movement and yet there were no reflections, just a wide stretch of pale grey water. On our way up Boshill I noticed a very large flat fungus growing at right-angles from a tree stump *(see page 8)*. It looked very much like a Beefsteak Fungus but I forgot to look at it on the way home. The wild flowers are lovely and I still marvel at their abundance this year. The roadsides, hedgerows and fields are a mass of colour and variation in plant life. Agrimony, St John's Wort *(see page 117)*, Field Scabious *(see page 112)*, Clover, Betony *(see page 113)* and both the Pink and White Yarrow.

16th July. A beautiful sunset of wispy pink and cream clouds like drifts of fine gauze over a blue and grey sky.

17th July. It has been a very warm, still day and this evening we went to Whitford Weir where it was pleasantly cool by the river.

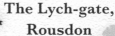

The Lych-gate, Rousdon

Common
Mullein

Common
Cat's ear

Marjoram

St. John's
Wort
(see 15th July)

Hedge
Bedstraw

Purple Toadflax

Common Centaury

The Old Water-mill *(see 26th July)*

There were some large Burdock *(see page 10)* plants, the hooked flower heads still green and soft yet they attached themselves to my clothes as I passed. The Teasels were in flower and I found a huge plant of the weird looking Figwort which had horrid fat brown grubs feeding on nearly every leaf. The rushes are out, the Water Forget-Me-Nots *(see this page)* and the Marsh Woundwort *(see page 106)* with the Hedge Woundwort I found a few weeks ago. In the hedges there were the white blossoms of Wild Privet and Lady's Bedstraw.

19th July. A single Black Headed Gull came to feed on the roof today, the first to visit us although there are quite a number about the river. I could not see the baby Seagulls anywhere. I am sure they are too young to fledge and wonder what has happened to them. Mr Seagull was very aggressive towards Mrs Seagull, which is most unusual. A particularly beautiful sunset this evening but impossible to describe.

BABY SEAGULLS

20th July. I could hear the squeaky whistle of the baby Seagulls this morning and found one perched on the lower dormer of their roof. It was quite large and speckled and still had some of its baby fluff. I couldn't see the other two but they must be around somewhere. We found a large beetle in James' bedroom and identified it as a Summer Cockchafer *(see page 113)*. It appeared to be dormant and seemed quite harmless so I put it on the land next door. A lovely little hen House Sparrow perched on our bird bath today – nothing spectacular, but she looked so pretty, all soft and round. This evening there were great, dark steely-grey and peach -pink clouds billowing out across a clear bright blue sky.

22nd July. There was another spectacular sunset as we returned from Uplyme this evening. Great shafts of golden orange light shone down from behind dark clouds mellowing the countryside with its warm glow.

Rush & Water Forget-me-not
(see 18th July)

23rd July. The baby Seagull has found its way on to our roof and after fluttering about for a while managed to fly onto the parapet. The parents watched anxiously from the chimney stack or wheeled above, screeching and diving to attack when anyone other than myself went on to the roof. For some time the baby teetered on the edge in the strong wind and it was hilarious to see it occasionally take off only to hover with its funny knobbly legs stretched out uneasily ready to find its feet. It was just like someone learning to swim needing the reassurance of the presence of terra firma. Eventually a gust of wind took it away and it half flew, half glided down to the beach where it ran about in a great state of agitation. During the day the wind freshened and the sea turned rough as low cloud came down over the cliffs bringing rain and much colder weather.

24th July. The heather is in full bloom on Woodbury Common.

26th July. Today I walked to the old Water Mill *(see page 118)* via Tapper's Knapp, past the thatched cottages and along the narrow path through the trees with the sound of the stream in the hollow. The hedges become high on each side until it reaches the gate into the Mill Field. The Mill is possibly 16th Century and still in working order although the wheel is only turned occasionally to keep it from rotting. The water is channelled down to the wheel in a stone gully and there is a small pool where the trout lie. I was told that the last miller went to the 1914-18 war and was killed and it has not been worked as a business since then. It is a lovely place to sit and paint with the sound of the water, the ducks busy dabbling in the stream and goats tethered further along the bank. The sun was hot but a cool breeze kept

Hermit Crab   **Sea Belt** *(see 1st July)*

**Serrated or
Toothed Wrack**

Spiny Cockle

**Sea Lettuce
Bladder Wrack** *(see 1st July*

it pleasant and drove away the flies. Brian brought home a large formation of pink coral dredged up by one of the fishermen. It smelt very strong so he washed it under the tap and out crawled great numbers of tiny crabs and sea creatures.

27th July. Quite a number of plants have established themselves on the rubble of the cliff fall and already it is overgrown in places with dense green foliage and bright flowers. The fields along the top of the cliff are beginning to turn brown owing to the lack of rain.

28th July. It remained humid all day and heavy cloud hung over the cliffs, faint sunlight occasionally breaking through to illuminate them. By evening dense misty rain-clouds were rolling down into the valley from the West and the wind freshened considerably. The brilliant blue green sea swept in with large waves breaking on the beach and at 11 p.m. thunder and lightning started followed by torrential rain soon afterwards.

29th July. There was heavy cloud obliterating the cliff tops early this morning and much rain, but the sun broke through and it looked like being a beautiful day. The overnight rain has left the countryside fresh and fragrant with the Honeysuckle still lovely in the hedge but the Wild Roses about over. I found some Wood Sage *(see pages 14 and 112)* and the first Tansy and a dead flower that was hard to identify but could have been Goats Beard. The Camomile is out and there are some fine specimens of Thistle *(see page 106)*, about five different species but I doubt if the gardener would appreciate their presence. The flowers of Traveller's Joy are out in profusion but are very insignificant compared to their fluffy Autumn cascades. When we descended Boshill at midday the distant hills were misty and grey with rain but in the valley the fields were brilliant yellow and green with sunshine. The evening was beautiful, warm grey and pink clouds radiant in the fading light as a crescent moon slipped into the sky, suspended in space. Yet there was a sombre note, as just offshore they were searching for a parachutist who had disappeared in the rough water. The closing of a day and the fading away of another life.

31st July. A wild and windy night followed by sunshine and some rain during the day. The wind was strong off the sea and the waves rough on the shore as great clouds moved across the sky.

August

Wispy clouds and calm, still water,
Hear the sigh of gentle waves,
Through the countryside to wander,
Harvest time and holidays.

Margaret I. Pogson

Portland Bill Lighthouse *(see 11th Aug.)*

AUGUST

1st Aug. A cold wind off the sea tonight and dark stormy clouds scudding across the moon.

2nd Aug. Mrs Seagull appears to have something wrong with her foot, keeping it tucked up underneath her and not letting it touch the ground. She has great difficulty trying to drink from the bird-bath as she stands on the edge on one leg.

GOLDEN LIGHTS

3rd Aug. The most beautiful clouds billowing across the sky today, bringing light rain showers with only odd snatches of sunshine. At 10.30 p.m. the evening light was still in the Western sky. The moon cast a distant golden reflection on the sea and by the shore there danced on the water a myriad of golden lights like sparks from a sparkler. By midnight only a faint light from the moon could be seen as sinister dark clouds covered its face. As I stood on the roof taking in the beauty of the sky and the sound of the sea, I could smell the scent of the Stocks in the front garden below.

4th Aug. Had a lovely fat Bumble Bee in the kitchen today and a Cabbage White Butterfly which is quite unusual with us being so high up. This evening a very hazy moon shed its silvery light in a shimmering path across the sea.

5th Aug. A very heavy mist this morning that soon cleared to reveal a bright, sunny day. During the afternoon I noticed yet another effect of light on the sea. The water was quite grey and broken but not rough with waves and sparkled all over with light.

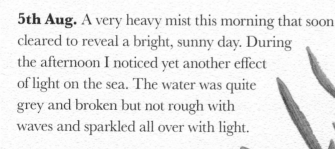

Samphire *(see 11th Aug.)*

The roadsides now appear
to be turning towards Autumn
with only greenery and seed heads to be
seen, although on closer inspection one can find the
flowers hidden by the long grass. Today I picked Centaury,
Ragwort and Nipplewort, Hawkbit, Hemp Agrimony *(see page 128)*
and the tiny Creeping Cinquefoil *(see page 107)*. There was a lovely brown
Butterfly fluttering about the grass and many Bees on the Great Willow Herb.
The Red Valerian *(see page 113)* is out in great profusion again this year but the
plants growing out of the walls at Axmouth are so sturdy, I can never quite make
up my mind whether they are wild or a cultivated variety.

6th Aug. Low cloud over the cliffs from early morning and generally a drizzly,
wet day. The baby Seagulls are now quite large and very speckled. They are
often on the roof and there is such a commotion if strangers approach them, the
parent birds screaming and swooping low to ward off any impending danger.

By evening the weather had cleared and the sun came
out. At sunset, dark clouds tinged with pink
were silhouetted against a bright pink
and blue sky, tinting all the
surrounding countryside.

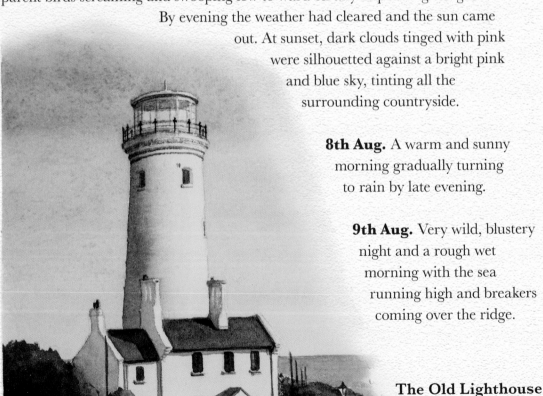

8th Aug. A warm and sunny
morning gradually turning
to rain by late evening.

9th Aug. Very wild, blustery
night and a rough wet
morning with the sea
running high and breakers
coming over the ridge.

**The Old Lighthouse
– Portland Bill**
(see 11th Aug.)

INTO DORSET

11th Aug. Went to Dorchester via Bridport and back along the coast road from Portland Bill. The landscape in Dorset is so different. The steeply rolling hills and patchwork of fields every shade of green from bright apple to sage, all broken with the lines of hedgerows and dotted with trees. Here and there a rounded hilltop crowned majestically with a little group of trees somehow managing to survive despite their exposed positions. The harvest is ripe, great fields of golden velvet falling before the combines. It was a warm, golden evening at Portland Bill with a cool, gentle breeze from the sea. I could sit for hours watching the force of the water breaking against the vast craggy rocks and sweeping along the smooth flat shelves. No sheltered haven her for the fishing boats but derricks to swing them out into the deep waters. Portland Lighthouse *(see page 124)* towered above with its brilliant red band, solid and firm against the storms, the surrounding stony grasslands dotted with clumps of Burdock, Restharrow *(see below)*, Sea Pinks and Samphire *(see page 125)*. We passed the Old Lighthouse *(see page 126)*, a cluster of charming buildings further along the coast and then homeward, the magnificent view of Chesil beach sweeping its way Westward into the sunset. The beauty of it all, the mellow thatched stone cottages, the evening sun on St Catherine's Chapel perched on the hill at Abbotsbury, the lines of fences casting long dark shadows on a glowing landscape. The ever-changing sky of evening, deep grey and pink, brilliant orange and gold enhanced the distant pale blue-grey cliffs and sea and the shimmering golden light on the water tracing the coastline beneath Golden Cap.

13th Aug. A very wet morning, turning wild and stormy with furious seas lashing the beach all day. By evening the wind had reached gale force but it remained mild. Such a foul night makes one appreciate being indoors tucked up in bed, dry and warm.

FASTNET TRAGEDY

14th Aug. Many casualties at sea last night in the Fastnet Yacht Race. The worst gales ever recorded for August. Raging seas and blustery winds all through the night and well into the morning. The horizon a dark navy blue and great towering green waves crashing down in clouds of spume, roaring and hissing along the shore. Gradually it abated by late afternoon.

Restharrow
(see 11th Aug.)

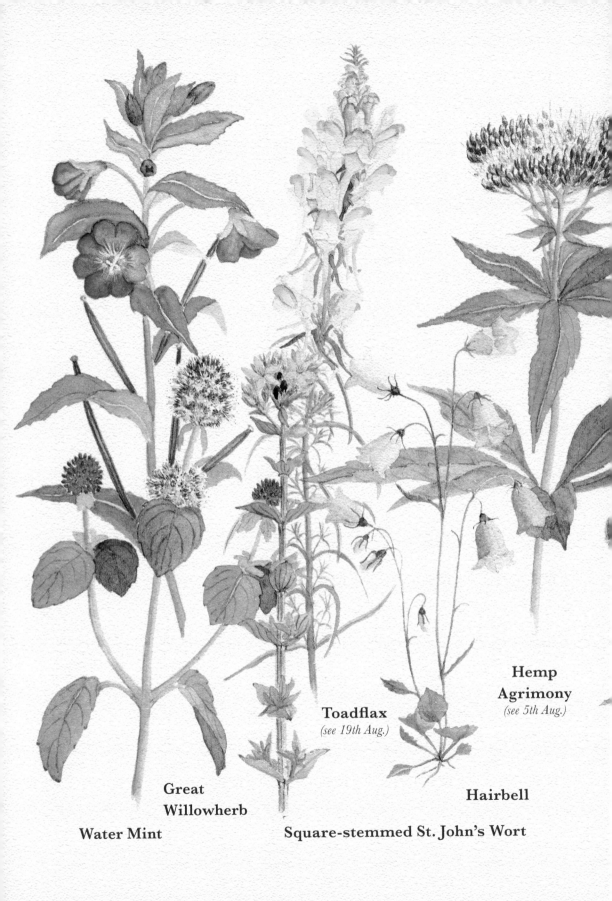

Hemp
Agrimony
(see 5th Aug.)

Toadflax
(see 19th Aug.)

Great
Willowherb

Hairbell

Water Mint

Square-stemmed St. John's Wort

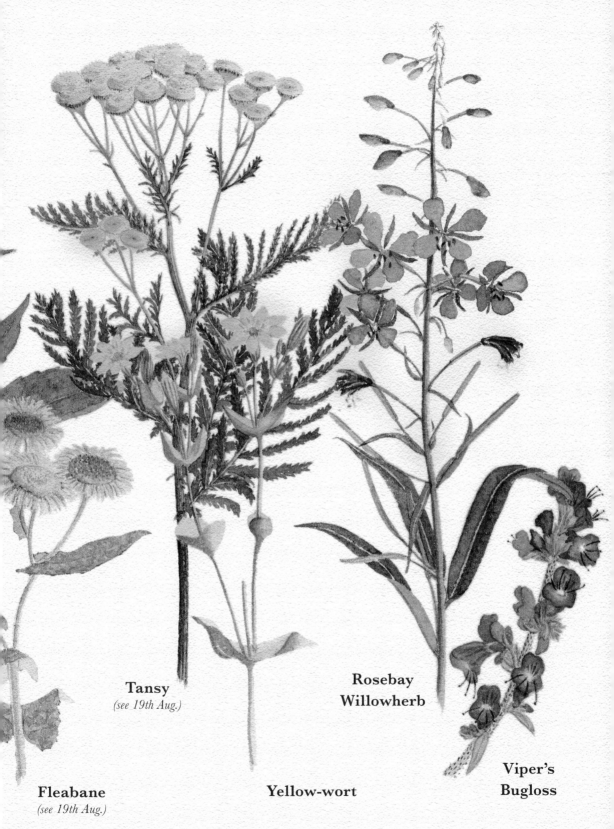

Tansy
(see 19th Aug.)

**Rosebay
Willowherb**

**Viper's
Bugloss**

Fleabane
(see 19th Aug.)

Yellow-wort

Shute House   **Landscape from Boshill**

15th Aug. After the ferocity of yesterday's storm brilliant sunshine and calmer seas greeted us this morning although the wind was still blowing hard and cold from the S.W. The sunset was fiery pink and violet, glowing ominously on the horizon with a pale eerie light.

16th Aug. Beer Regatta Sailing Race today with white sails all across the bay this morning but the sea turned rough and the wind freshened, whipping up white horses. By mid-afternoon it was wild and stormy again with the rain beating against the windows.

17th Aug. This evening the whole Seagull family turned up to be fed. To our great surprise there was a third baby although it didn't appear to associate with the others. The large speckled fledglings squeaked and whistled, prodding their parents, expecting to be fed. It looked so incongruous as they were nearly as large as their parents. It was lovely to see them all together as a family, safely reared and healthy.

Musbury Castle

CHILDHOOD MEMORIES

19th Aug. Early this morning I went to the top of Trow Hill to look at
a field of stooks *(see page 132)*. It was a very nostalgic scene reminding me
of my childhood days when the war was on and we would go gleaning for the
odd ears of wheat left by the reaper. Farmers would allow us to gather them
in sackfuls for our chickens and we would spend back-breaking hours picking
them up from between the sheaves. Mother would come with a billy-can of
tea and some cake and we would sit in the shade of a hedge, thankful for the
chance of a rest. There was peace and tranquillity in that small corner of
a field in the still heat of the afternoon. The wheat grown today has a much
shorter stem which is damaged by modern methods of harvesting, so long-
stem varieties are grown by a few farmers specially for thatching. Once again
the neat rows of stooks add the air of tidiness and order of a bygone age.

The Field of Stooks *(see 19th Aug.)*

Sheep were grazing on
the opposite hillside, woolly
bundles dotted over the bright green
fields. Autumn is slowly creeping up
on us. The roadsides have lost their fresh
greenness, the brilliant banks of wild
flowers having faded leaving fluffy heads
of Thistledown and the outlines of Hogweed
heavy with seeds. Here and there a dying leaf
gleams golden and the splash of scarlet berries
of ripening Lords-and-Ladies show themselves
brilliantly against the fading foliage. The Toadflax
(see page 128) is in flower at Ware Cross and
there are still a few fading Ragwort.
The yellow of Fleabane *(see page 129)* and
Tansy *(see page 129)*
brightens the scene,
with the subdued-pinky heads
of Hemp Agrimony. The brambles are
thick with pink and white blossom and
the Hips and Haws are fat and green.
The view from the top of Seaton Down
Hill was magnificent, the pale stretch of sea
in the early morning light and the undulating
hills around Axmouth a patchwork of fields,
here and there golden with harvest amongst
the pastureland.

21st Aug. The evening was mild and still. The pale
cream Cumulus clouds on the Northern horizon were
tinged with pink and reminded me of the Jungfrau at
sunset. We were at Seaton Hole as night settled, sitting
quietly listening to the chirp of Crickets and the sound
of waves on the beach below. It was a clear, dark night,
the stars twinkling brightly and far away at Portland Bill
we could see the flash of the light.

**Wheat, Oats, Barley
and Scentless Mayweed**

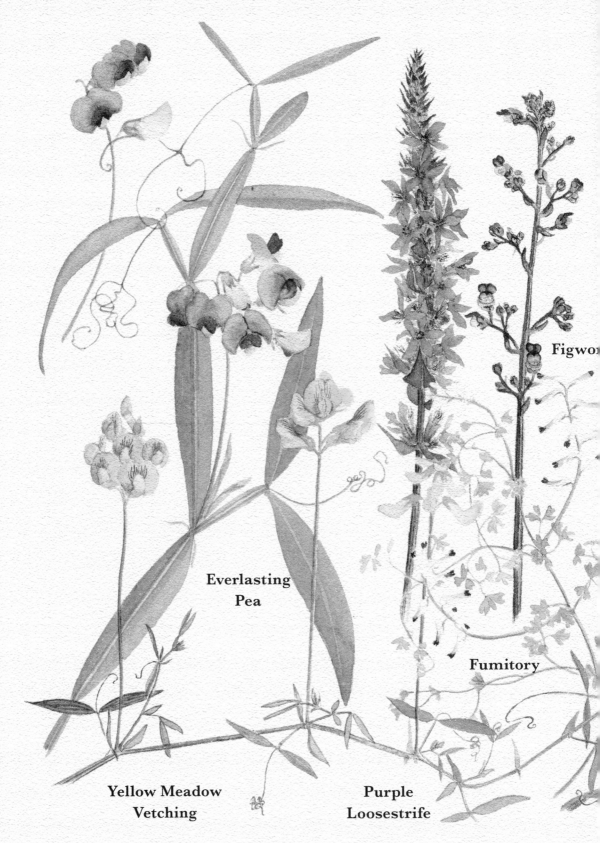

Everlasting
Pea

Figwor

Fumitory

Yellow Meadow
Vetching

Purple
Loosestrife

134

24th Aug. After two days of sunshine and heavy showers we woke this morning to stormy weather from the S.W. The bay was a beautiful deep blue and green broken with little white horses and great clear green waves rolled in onto the shore.

25th Aug. Very wet for most of the day and much cooler. There was the most beautiful sunset over the Axe Valley. The dark, heavy clouds of late evening and the distant hills were silhouetted against a deep peach-pink sky, deepening as the light faded. The wide expanse of water at high tide and the curves of the river higher up the valley were a pure, pale, silvery-pink.

MISTY MORNING

27th Aug. A pale blue misty morning with a warm glow of early sunlight on the cliffs and a heavy mist over the marshes. The sea quite still, just lazily undulating against the shore. What had promised to be a beautiful day turned quite cloudy by mid-morning, the little fluffy clouds all across the sky, joining up to blot out the sun. However, it cleared by midday and at 2.15 p.m. I set out to walk the 2 ½ miles along the beach past Culverhole Point to the wreck of the *Fairway*. It was hazy and hot, the towering

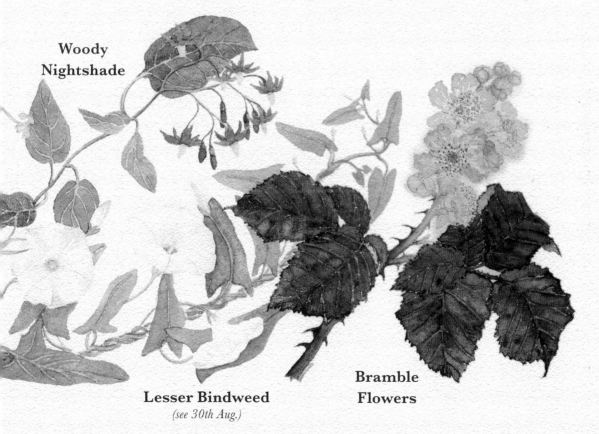

Woody Nightshade

Lesser Bindweed
(see 30th Aug.)

Bramble Flowers

The Wreck of the *Fairway* (*see 27th Aug.*)

sandstone cliffs reflecting the heat of the sun. At first it was easy going on the firm sand and flat rocks. Oystercatchers and Gulls were feeding along the shoreline and there were great numbers of Mussels which had been thrown up the beach by the severe storms, then opened and eaten by the sea birds. The sand gave way to large shingle shifting under my feet as I walked and then great rocks which made it necessary to pick my way carefully. In many places, the cliff had fallen leaving great boulders on the beach and clumps of Purple Loosewife, Fleabane and Camomile growing down to the shingle.

THE SHIPWRECK

The wreck is quite massive, far larger than I ever imagined and tragic to see, silently rusting and rotting away *(see page 136)*. The bridge streaked with rust, the hull remarkably sound but driven well up the beach and firmly embedded by the February storms. She went aground on 2nd December, 1978 after dragging her anchors. Her engine had failed and the Torbay Lifeboat - *Edward Bridges*, took off the six man crew, the Coxswain later being awarded the R.N.L.I. Bronze Medal for the rescue. We caught a brief glimpse of her at about 7.30 a.m., a ghostly grey form, her lights barely visible through the driving spray and wild, stormy seas. When we looked again a moment later, she had disappeared. Water from a spring in the cliffs, cascaded over the slabs of Blue Lias nearby and collected in large crystal-clear pools along the beach. It was much cooler when I set out for the long trek home but the tide had come in covering the sand and small stones so I had to trudge along on the rough shingle for most of the way. Tiny streams of water trickled down the cliff face, the sunlight turning them to silver. When I stopped to rest I found two very interesting stones, on the end of one the fossilised print of a scallop shell and the other a piece of sedimentary strata, Blue Lias in the middle and white crystalline rock at each end. I hope to return soon to explore the rock-pools and make a more detailed study of the beach.

30th Aug. Despite a chill in the air and a heavy mist early this morning, the glorious weather continues. I went to the old Mill again today. As I sat painting the tethered Nanny Goat grazed nearby, occasionally calling to her kids, ducks dabbled in the stream and hens scratched about amongst the grass, stopping to drink from my water jar. I was quite content just to sit listening to the birds and the sound of the stream rippling over the stones on that warm still morning. The pale pink flowers of Lesser Bindweed *(see page 135)* threaded their way through the hedgerow, turning their faces to the sun with the last few flowers of Summer.

31st Aug. A very heavy mist hung around from early morning with the hills above Axmouth and the cliffs barely visible, just ghostly out-lines above the marshes and the sea. It became quite dense and persisted well into the afternoon until slowly it was suffused with a beautiful soft light which shimmered over the pale grey sea. The last day of August and Autumn slowly settles over the countryside. The mornings and evenings are cold and damp and the nights begin to draw in. Already it is quite dark by 8.30 p.m.

Home with the catch

September

Autumn Fruits are slowly ripening,
Harvest safely gathered in,
Cobwebs bright with dewdrops sparkling,
Blackberries and mushrooming.

Margaret I. Pogson

Early Evening on the Beach *(see 11th Sept.)*

SEPTEMBER

1st Sept. Misty, dull and humid for most of the day with just a fleeting spell of sunshine in the late afternoon. The wind freshened during the evening bringing light rain. The baby seagulls still pester their parents for food and one in particular still hangs around Mrs Seagull, prodding her and squeaking pathetically and yet it should be quite capable of fending for itself *(see below)*. Poor Mrs Seagull is moulting and looks very weary, with baby following her wherever she goes.

2nd Sept. Heavy rain last night washed away the dust and the dirt from the countryside leaving it fresh and green in the morning sun. I picked the flowers of Old Man's Beard *(see page 149),* the pretty trails of Goose Grass quite dainty and tinged with red and the berries of the Wayfaring tree *(see page 143)*. The Blackberries are ripening and the Honeysuckle berries glow like jewels in the hedgerows with the bright orange clusters of Lords and Ladies *(see page 148)*. There are still many beautiful plants to find but one has to look a little more closely.

4th Sept. The weather remains mild and humid with just occasional sunshine breaking through the clouds and the sea is still and glassy.
Tonight the moon is full and shines out across the
water with dark clouds etched against
its brilliance a drifting mistily
across its face.

**Feeding
Baby**

(see 1st Sept.)

Hornbeam

Beech
(see 13th Sept.)

Elder
(see 30th Sept.)

Ash
(see 20th Sept.)

Snowberry

Woody
Nightshade

Crab Apples
(see 29th May)

Honeysuckle

Sycamore

Rowan
*(see 20th
Sept.)*

Hazel
(see 13th Sept.)

Dogwood
(see 7th Nov.)

Wayfaring Tree
(see 13th Sept.)

5th Sept. A hot, humid day with brilliant sunshine and blue sky. I walked down the Marsh Path to pick more Travellers' Joy, Healbane and Mugwort *(see page 10)*. The Haws are turning red and the Blackberries there are plump and ripe. Growing on the rough land were a number of Shaggy Ink-Caps which looked quite revolting *(see page 148)*. Some years ago I came across a much taller species of this fungi, each about 15 ins high and spilling its inky-black fluid in long drips to the ground. They encircled a rough grave in a cemetery and I will never forget that macabre scene – it was worthy of any horror film. By evening the wind was blowing cold from the North and a blue haziness settled over the sea and cliffs against a backcloth of misty pink sky.

6th Sept. Thick fog this morning with the edge of the beach barely visible and when I opened the window the chill damp air smelt of Autumn. It was nearly midday before it cleared and by then the sun was hot but there was a cold wind off the sea. The brilliant reflection of light from the broken surface of the water was dazzling, an incredible sea of dancing, flashing silver.

8th Sept. On our way to Axminster today along the Musbury Road we noticed a number of trees with silvery foliage. As we could not remember seeing them like that before we thought perhaps they were dying until we passed them and could see the leaves were the usual green. We then realised they were White Poplars *(see page 145)*, the white felt-like underside of the leaves showing in the Southerly wind.

Pale yellow Toadflax clustered along the road side and on our way home at Whitford Weir there were great banks of Indian Balsam *(see page 144)*.

9th Sept. This morning the coastline to Portland was clearly visible stark grey against a low formation of brilliant pink clouds. One could distinctly follow the rise and fall of the land to the highest point and the slope away to the sea at Portland Bill.

Indian Balsam *(see 8th Sept.)*

144

11th Sept. I awoke at 3 a.m. and it was so quiet I crept out
of bed and looked through the window. It was a most beautiful
night, the sea quite still and the twinkling lights of a ship shone
brightly on the horizon. All was bathed in the pale silvery glow
of moonlight. The morning was fine with bright sunshine over
the sea turning the cliffs to gold and a faint mist hung over the
marshes. Heavy clouds formed during the day but the sun
often broke through. Later I sat on the beach and as I watched
the evening close in, grey clouds tinged with pink gradually
cleared leaving deep blue sky above fading to pale pinky-grey on the
horizon. The fishermen are already preparing to leave the beach for the
Winter and were busy with their boats *(see page 140)*.

**White
Poplar**
(see 8th Sept.)

13th Sept. The early morning was very overcast with a menacing pink glow
in the sky to the N.E. and heavy cloud moving in from the West. However, I had
arranged to walk the Landslip Path with a friends and by 10.20 a.m. we were on our
way from Ware Cross. In places the lane was thick with Beech Mast *(see page 142)* that had
already fallen. We passed the gate leading to Ware Cliffs and could see the lovely stretch
of coastline Eastwards to Golden Cap. Then we reached the beginning of the path and
so began the six mile walk through the cliffs to Seaton. Such stillness and peace with
barely the stirring of a leaf or twitter of a bird. For most of the way the path is narrow,
rising and falling, twisting and turning by hollows and chasms and towering rock faces.
We reached a clearing with two beautiful Beech Trees, the earth carpeted with the rich
russet of fallen leaves. At Rousdon we stopped to rest on a cliff top, the land Eastward
falling away to Charton Bay *(see pages 146/147)* and high Sandstone cliffs to the West.

The Landslip Cottage
*(see page vii &
13th Sept.)*

Charton Bay *(see 13th Sept.)*

LANDSLIP COTTAGE

The sun came out brilliant in a clear blue sky but we could catch only a brief glimpse of it as the trees thinned out overhead, the shafts of light shining down to illuminate bright patches of foliage and the fronds of Ferns. Then on through the remains of the great landslip that occurred on Christmas Day 1839, passing the place where the Landslip Cottage once stood *(see pages vii/145)*. I remember it well as I was taken there as a child on a number of occasions by my Father to see 'Auntie Mary', my Great Aunt. She lived in the beautiful thatched cottage and kept a rustic tea-garden in the cliffs. Every week she would go to Axminster by

train to buy provisions, walking all the way home from Combpyne
Station through Dowlands, with a yoke over her shoulders to take
the heavy loads. She wore a dark ankle-length dress and I remember
seeing her sitting by the great open fireplace, the ovens underneath at
floor level and a large black kettle swinging from a hook. Driftwood
was gathered from the beach for fuel and fresh water came from a
spring in the garden. Her daughter Annie Gapper lived with her and
they remained there during the war although the cliff was mined.
When the old lady died aged 93 in 1950, Annie moved away and the
cottage was mysteriously burned down. Exposed to the weather and
encroachment of undergrowth it finally disappeared and now there
is nothing to mark the once famous landmark.

We continued along the path, everywhere trees reaching for the sky, clambering, and underfoot, the soft foam of rotting leaves. There were Sloes, the berries of Honeysuckle and Wayfaring Tree *(see page 143)*, clusters of bright yellow and green Crab Apples and Sweet Chestnuts *(see page 168)*. I found the papery flowers of a long dead plant and the most beautiful shiny green Bryony berries trailing in perfect formation through the bushes. The Squirrels had been busy with the Hazel Nuts *(see page 143)*, but had left only empty shells for us to break open. The ground was littered with the remnants of last Winter's store and the new creamy nuts in their bright green husks but all had been nibbled by sharp teeth. The path opened out onto a rocky outcrop and we stopped for a late picnic lunch, the sun blazing down but a pleasant cool breeze from the sea. The narrow path continued on then suddenly climbing steeply we found ourselves on the soft springy turf of the open cliff top. Over a stile and along the edge of the fields, the stubble from a field of oats glowing golden in the sunlight, I came across a fine plant of Viper's Bugloss but the flowers were nearly over. Down the narrow track between the hedges we went, then home across the golf course, stopping for a moment to lean on a gate to admire the distant-view of the rolling Devonshire countryside, the greens and golds of the fields paling to the blues and greys of faraway hills.

TO PLYMOUTH

14th Sept. Another warm sunny day but a distinct nip in the early morning air. On our way to Plymouth we could see the distinct brown patterned moors, the Tors stark against the sky, the wide silver water of the Exe and the ship that is always moored in the same place whenever we pass the Exeter Canal. We passed farmsteads tucked away in hollows and the glassy expanse of water of the Plym estuary at high tide. On our way home I noticed the stooks had been gathered in at the top of Trow Hill and made into a solitary 'haystack' in the corner of the field *(see page 149)*. A glowing golden sunset with the dark violet-grey clouds of evening tinged with pink filled the sky.

Lords and Ladies *(see 2nd Sept.)*
Shaggy Ink-Cap *(see 5th Sept.)*

Goosegrass

**Flowers of
Old Man's
Beard**
(see 2nd Sept.)

15th Sept. A fine morning with
the mist drifting over the surface
of the sea tinted by the sun and a clear
sky lightly streaked with clouds.
The mornings are now quite chilly
and the air smells of Autumn which
seems to bring a quiet subdued
stillness to the sea. The sun is
still hot in sheltered places but
the chill wind makes one begin
to think of finding warmer clothes.

Corn Rick
(see 14th Sept.)

The Blacksmiths at Branscombe *(see 29th Sept.)*

16th Sept. This morning, from the bedroom window to the South, I could see bright sunshine and clear blue sky over the rough deep blue-green sea and yet when I went down to the kitchen, facing North, there appeared another world. The whole of the Axe valley was enveloped in misty grey cloud tinted with the sombre pink of the sky and it looked as though any moment heavy rain would descend upon us. But it cleared, leaving a beautiful sunny day. The last of the harvest is being gathered in around Dowlands and Axmouth and I realised today the Swallows are no longer about. The Swifts left some time ago but it is a little early for the Swallows – they are probably congregating on the telephone wires somewhere.

17th Sept. A light ethereal mist drifted over the marshes this morning silhouetting the higher ground and distant trees, the picture of a world that somehow wasn't quite reality. The wind freshened again during the day and turned much colder yet the pale blue-grey mist of Autumn remained. The deep grey clouds of evening over White Cliff were split horizontally, great shafts of light shining through from a pale pink sky.

18th Sept. The wind strengthened considerably during the night and by morning rough deep blue-green seas were churning in although it had turned mild. I went by train to Southampton. The railway banks are still bright with flowers, Wild Pea, Toadflax, Balsam and Golden Rod. The last of the harvest has been gathered in and great areas have been fired to burn away the golden stubble and yet the blackened land is already showing fresh green growth. The farmers are busy ploughing, turning over the rich deep soil in preparation for the next crop. In the parks the leaves are turning gold and brown and the Horse Chestnuts are shedding their 'Conkers'. We admired the beautiful bark of the Silver Birch and twisted trunk of the Sweet Chestnut. The sky remained overcast all day and after a few light showers, the rain set in.

Shoeing *(see 29th Sept.)*

Woodbury Common *(see 20th Sept.)*

19th Sept. A dismal, dreary day with mild blustery winds and low cloud over the cliffs. Frequent heavy rain spread it's greyness across the marshes.

VIEWS FROM WOODBURY COMMON

20th Sept. A dazzling golden sunrise outlined Haven Cliff and reflected with such brilliance from the sea it was quite blinding. We went to paint on Woodbury Common. The 'haystack' at the top of Trow Hill has been thatched and is worthy of more than a passing glance. So much has gone into its creation since the sowing of the seed. We stopped at Newton Poppleford to collect some fire-wood and in a field opposite were some Sows and a number of lovely pink Piglets, all thoroughly enjoying themselves rooting about. It was a fine day, the view over the Exe to the distant hills of Dartmoor clear and bright in the morning sun and clouds billowing across the sky *(see page 152)*. Beautiful dry grasses blew in the wind amongst the yellow flowers of the Gorse and I picked Heather and Ling *(see page 153)*. The soft afternoon sunlight mellowed all the colours of the countryside, the distant trees and shrubs, the Bracken and Heather and the changing leaves of Autumn. The Ash *(see page 142)* keys and bright Rowan berries *(see page 143)* hung thickly in the trees and far away, beyond it all, the pale silvery horizon of the sea. The ploughs were busy, once again exposing the rich red soil, followed by great white flocks of Gulls wheeling and diving and settling to feed from the newly turned earth. We returned home passing the field's patterned with the stripes of burnt stubble and clumps of large-flowered Evening Primrose *(see page 106)* growing by the roadside.

22nd Sept. The morning was fine and sunny but by midday the sky had become overcast. Towards late afternoon the sky to the North was filled with dark thundery clouds illuminated by bright sunshine from the South. The hills on the distant horizon were a deep subdued blue. A fresh cold wind blew up from the North and deep grey billowing clouds tinged with pink spread themselves right along the Southern horizon over the sea.

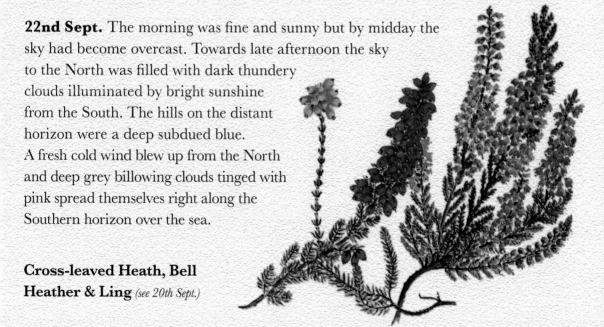

Cross-leaved Heath, Bell Heather & Ling *(see 20th Sept.)*

Boat-builders *(see 24th Sept.)*

Yew
(see 25th Sept.)

23rd Sept. Early this morning the sea was as still as a mill-pond, with a dark blue horizon but the wind rose to become blustery and cold from the North. Many people spoke of a frost this morning but the minimum temperature on the roof last night was 35 degrees Fahrenheit. Beautiful sunshine lasted all day although it remained cold even when the wind had abated. Today I saw the first crisp brown leaves blowing along the road – alas Autumn is upon us!

24th Sept. I went to the boat builders this morning. They were working on a 21 ft. Clinker built boat of Elm on Oak *(see page 168)* and what a joy it was to see the massive timbers of the keel and bilge-ways, the curve of the ribs, the smoothness of the wood and glint of copper nails. The strength of its craftsmanship, the grace and symmetry of its lines made it a fine sturdy craft of great beauty and truly a work of art *(see pages 154/155)*. This evening there were a number of very sinister dark grey clouds above Beer Head, one rectangular in shape and quite vertical. I saw a Grey Squirrel running along the side of the road near Boshill Cross.

DARTMOOR

25th Sept. We went to Dartmoor today, to Haytor. After leaving Bovey Tracey the road began to climb and everywhere there were Rowan Trees, scarlet with berries. It was quite a steep walk over the short springy turf between Bracken, Heather and Gorse to the dark mass of weather-worn rock at the top of Haytor. As well as the sheep and shaggy Dartmoor Ponies *(see page 157)*, I was surprised to find Cattle grazing there. Some had quite young calves with them, their coats thick and curly. The view from the top was magnificent, the vast sweep of the moor broken with rocky outcrops and distant Tors, the thin curve of the road disappearing over the moor and all the patterned fields, gold and red and green merging to an indistinct blur of blue mistiness with sky and sea *(see page 158)*.

DARTINGTON

From there we went onto Dartington College of Arts, the road following the River Dart and the Dart Valley Railway, for part of the way. We spent the rest of the afternoon walking in the grounds. The gardens are so beautiful, fine trees and terraces, steps and paths and a curved stone seat above the sweep of the lawns. So many greens against a backcloth of bright yellow stubble in the fields nearby. Magnolias were in flower and a species of Chinese tree was covered with sweetly scented blossom. The Autumn Crocus spread their pale mauve blooms beneath the Beeches and here and there a Golden leaf fluttered to the ground. The Yew berries were ripening, like pale pink wax and the Sweet Chestnuts were laden with the spikey husks of the nuts. I found some Beech Mast attached to its twig, the shell split and showing the nuts nestling inside. A Grey Squirrel scuttled across the grass, its bushy tail trailing behind it.

It was evening when we left and as the light faded the clouds became heavier settling over the Tors in all the most beautiful shades of grey tinted with pink. The whole landscape glowed in its reflection. Slowly, the sky to the West cleared to a lovely shade of pale turquoise and pink with the dark edge of the evening sky etched against it and streaked with long clouds of brilliant orange. The sunset continued to change, the dark night clouds slowly moving across the sky until one narrow band of pale orange light remained. Then darkness, with just the twinkling lights of the town in the valley below.

Dartmoor Ponies *(see 25th Sept.)*

Dartmoor – View from Haytor *(see 25th Sept.)*

BRANSCOMBE AND THE BLACKSMITH

29th Sept. I went to Branscombe today, through the narrow lanes from Beer. Such a lovely little village of well-kept cottages and a church that seems to have moulded itself into the side of the valley over the centuries. We passed the old thatched Forge where the blacksmith still shoes horses *(see pages 150/151)* and across the road the last remaining Bakehouse where the ovens are fired with Ash faggots. We climbed the steep path to the woods at the head of the valley and followed the track through fields until we came out on high ground above the church. At the edge of a field we sat in the warm sunshine and brewed up some tea in a flask. The path widened and we reached a sheltered spot with a wooden seat near the cliff edge. I looked down over rocky pinnacles, along the length of the beach to Beer Head and Westwards to Sidmouth. Beyond, the coastline was just a thin outline against the overcast sky. We followed the path down the cliff, behind the old Coastguard houses and by the stream through the fields. The water bubbled and gurgled over the stones and under tiny wooden bridges as cows sleepily chewed the cud in the meadows along the banks. The wind was cold on the cliff and yet there was a mildness in the sheltered places.

30th Sept. The morning was misty and damp with a cold wind on the exposed higher ground. We went to Uplyme and returned through Venlake, passing under Cannington Viaduct and along to Shapwick. There were not many Hazel Nuts but the Blackberries were ripe and juicy, their leaves beginning to turn a lovely shade of yellow edged with red. Shiny green Bryony berries trailed through the bushes and there were still some Foxgloves and trails of Honeysuckle tucked away in the hedges. I picked Oak Apples and found an Oak leaf 8 ¼ ins long. The Elders *(see page 142)* are laden with berries after masses of fragrant blossom in the early Summer and one spray of leaves was turning a beautiful magenta. Here and there in the hedgerows are splashes of colour, a single vivid leaf, sometimes a small tree or bush a pale shade of yellow or even pink and the gold and brown of Bracken against the remaining green foliage. They were busy ploughing in the top fields attracting the Gulls and numerous birds and we saw a Kestrel hovering in the sky.

October

Fat brown nuts and ripe red berries,
Leaves of russet, red and gold,
Weeks and months become just memories,
Alas, the year is growing old.

Margaret I. Pogson

High Tide *(see 24th Oct.)*

OCTOBER

1st Oct. A very cloudy, misty morning followed by a warm sunny day and clear blue skies. Tonight a beautiful moon is illuminating the sea, occasionally misting over with cloud.

2nd Oct. Very thick fog that slowly cleared but the sun came out only briefly before it clouded over again. We went to Exmouth and sat for a while on the seafront, watching the white crests of water breaking along the sand bar. Quite close to us two Gulls strutted around as though they owned the place. Across the estuary we could see the distant view of Dartmoor sombre with heavy cloud. We returned via Woodbury Common but the heavy mist obscured the view. The moisture was collecting like dew on the dense gossamer webs spun across the low Gorse bushes. I have never seen such a large area completely covered by cobwebs as to appear impenetrable. The bright red berries of Rowan and Honeysuckle were vivid in the hedgerows, golden Gorse, Heather and Ling adding to all the colours of the Autumn foliage. There were still some Toadflax and in one place on the roadside, a most beautiful show of Poppies. The Horse Chestnuts on Trow Hill and much of the Bracken are turning golden and russet *(see page 168)*. By evening it had started to drizzle and gradually turned to heavy rain.

3rd Oct. Thick fog again this morning until nearly midday when the sun broke through for a short while making it unbearably humid. Heavy mist soon gathered again and by evening it was raining. After a torrential downpour, the wind freshened, whistling and howling through the windows and the calm, silent sea of the last few days became stormy and wild.

4th Oct. An attempt was made to blow up the wreck today but I have heard it was not very successful. A beautiful wintry sunset with dark pink clouds from North to South against a blue and turquoise sky. It was one of those magical evenings, the night air cool and fresh, the gentle sound of the waves on the shore and the whole expanse of the sky clear and bright with moonlight and stars. I could see the lights along the coastline to Start Point, of passing ships on the horizon and Portland Bill.

Cannington Viaduct *(see 24th Oct./1st Nov.)*

Seaton from White Cliff *(see 9th Oct.)*

5th Oct. When I first looked out over the sea at about 7 a.m. this morning there was a most unusual formation of vertical grey clouds rising out of the mist and silhouetted against a dusky pink sky. After a glorious day of brilliant sunshine, the wind freshened during the evening, rattling the windows. Mr and Mrs Seagull appear to have left their rooftop home for more sheltered Winter quarters as I have not seen them around lately. When I put out some food today about six gulls flew down and started to fight over it which would not have happened had they still been here.

6th Oct. I woke early this morning and at about 5 a.m. I looked out to see brilliant moonlight illuminating the sea at Seaton Hole. The waves were churning in, one after another, a rolling mass of darkness, greyness and creamy white light. The dawn was golden and red, the outline of Haven Cliffs stark against the brilliant light. The cliffs at Beer Head were quite pink with a blue green sky above. I picked some Hops *(see page 168)* in

the hedgerows at Uplyme – at least, Brian picked them for me as I couldn't reach them. The Beech leaves were brown and gold and falling fast. All day the long crested surf rolled in and by late afternoon it was raining heavily. In the evening huge waves were sweeping up the beach well above the tide line and as we watched in the darkness we could see great numbers of white birds, flying out in to the storm. I went onto the roof to get a better view and saw flock after flock of them disappearing into the wild stormy night. I think they must have been migrating – I cannot think of any other reason for such small creatures to venture out across the sea in such treacherous weather.

7th Oct. Although a much quieter morning, the sea is still rough and clouds of misty spray drift across the beach. There is a lot of driftwood on the shore and a beautifully shaped green bottle which I have kept. This evening I could see a light on the beach under Haven Cliffs – no doubt an angler doing a spot of night fishing.

Guelder Rose

Horse Chestnut
(see 2nd Oct.)

Oak
(see 24th Sept.)

Blackthorn
(see 1st May)

Hops
(see 6th Oct.)

Maple
(see 2nd Jan.)

Purging Buckthorn

Hawthorn

Spindle

169

EXPLORING ROCK POOLS

9th Oct. I walked to Beer today, along the beach to Seaton Hole and then over the cliff. Such a lovely view from the top looking back over the wide sweep of the bay and the Axe Valley with Seaton nestling by the river estuary *(see pages 166/167)*. From the path we looked down the cliff face to the rocky beach below, the Pigeons and Gulls perched on the ledges and a tangle of scrub with Toadflax, Privet berries, Sloes and Blackberries *(see page 176)*. The sun was bright and warm when we reached Beer and we sat overlooking the cove, the fishing boats hauled up on the beach below us. We returned along the beach, the towering cliffs above us and in places deep cavities beneath them, worn into the rock by the action of the sea. There were rocks and boulders all along the beach and a pinnacle nearly separated from the cliff face. A massive area of rock appeared to be part of the cliff but had obviously fallen at some time as the strata ran at a completely different angle. Stepping from rock to rock I stopped here and there to search the pools and found the most interesting things. Transparent Shrimps were swimming about, a little green Sand Eel about 2 inches long, jade and brown Sea Anemones and a tiny Hermit Crab moving along with his shell home on his back *(see page 196/197)*. The tide was out, leaving the rocks covered in thick brown Seaweed, Limpets and Winkles and the air full of the smell of the sea *(see page 196/197)*. I watched a Shag diving, counting the seconds before it reappeared on the surface. On the grassy slopes at the top of the cliff were some fine specimens of Ink-Cap Fungi.

10th Oct. Heavy rain during the early part of the day and at night dark clouds scudding across the moon.

11th Oct. As evening fell the sky over Beer Head became a jumble of broken clouds all grey, blue and mauve against the bright evening light. A distant stretch of water under the cliffs was a pale icy blue contrasting vividly with the stormy grey-green of the rest of the sea.

12th Oct. A very wild green sea this morning with white crests tumbling all across the bay. Although rough and windy it remained mild. The tide was out when we went along by the Axe at about 4.30 p.m. and the whole of the mud flats were closely dotted with flocks of birds facing South into the wind. To see such vast numbers again, feeding at ebb-tide reminds me only too well that the wintry weather will soon be upon us. When we returned later the evening sun was a fiery ball low in the sky and the whole Southern horizon glowed with a menacing pink light surmounted by dark grey skies. By late evening it was raining heavily and we could see lightning out at sea. Yesterday many people at Lyme Regis saw a water-spout moving across the bay – a once in a lifetime experience. The barometer is falling fast.

13th Oct. A thick fog this morning but it soon lifted, the sun breaking through and the sky clearing by 11 a.m. As we drove along the Axe Valley we could see a very heavy grey cloud lying horizontally just above the ground from Musbury to Shute. It really looked quite odd as though anyone walking through it would have their head in the sunshine above and only their legs showing below. At Rousdon a large flock of Gulls were feeding in a pasture amongst the Cows grazing. One is used to seeing them following the plough but they looked very out of place pecking about in the grass. Such a beautiful day, warm sunshine, blue sky with occasional fleecy clouds but a distinct chill and smell of Autumn in the air. All around the colours of the countryside are fading; distances subdued in pale sunlight but here and there the vivid scarlet of Hips and Haws and the rich shades of gold, amber and russet of the bracken *(see page 176)*.

16th Oct. Early this morning there was a thick fog and the sea was so still it barely turned on the shore. Despite the weather we left for a day on Exmoor and as we crossed Honiton Common the sky cleared and the sun came out but we kept running into patches of fog and low cloud. The grass was covered with a heavy dew giving it a silvery blue appearance and all the cobwebs strung between the Gorse and Bracken were bright with dew drops glistening in the morning light. From Tiverton the road followed the

Exe Valley the river rippling swiftly over stones and winding its way through glades as the tree covered hills rose steeply around us. A pale-blue Autumn mist added a touch of mystery to it all. We stopped to watch a number of beautiful Cock Pheasants and Hens wandering about the main road, one sitting on a fence so close I could almost touch it.

TO EXMOOR: PORLOCK, TARR STEPS AND DULVERTON

We turned off at Wheddon Cross and went up to Dunkery Bridge hoping to walk to the top of Dunkery Beacon. On a fine day one can see across the Bristol Channel to the Welsh mountains but alas, the fog kept coming down so we only went a short way along the track. A little brook ran under a small stone bridge into a beautiful shallow pool overhung with Rowan and surrounded by short springy turf, rich russet and green Bracken and tiny plants. The road descended to Porlock, winding through shady woods the tall straight trees blotting out most of the light and sheltering the thick carpet of ferns which were still green. Across the road in the more open woodland they had turned such a bright yellow it was as though the sun was shining. At the top of Porlock Hill we took the road to Exford by Lucott Cross, occasionally catching a glimpse of the moor when the fog temporarily cleared. There were often Sheep at the roadside, the Rams with fine curled horns and some so tame they came if you spoke to them. From Winsford Hill we turned down to Tarr Steps, the bridge of the stone slabs, probably prehistoric, across the river Barle. Such a lovely tranquil place at this time of year, the wide river rippling gently over the stones, between deep wooded hillsides. We went through Dulverton then headed for home, a few lingering reminders of Summer along the way. A Foxglove, a group of Scarlet Poppies, clumps of Toadflax and some Campion. Heavy rain set in before we reached Seaton, the leaden sky suffused with pink.

18th Oct. After the early morning fog had lifted, the sun shone brilliantly from a clear blue sky for the rest of the day. We walked the Branscombe cliff path again but in reverse, through the lower fields by the steam and then into the cliff where we sat for three hours in the warm sunshine. The short

Tarr Steps (*see 16th Oct.*)

turf was quite dry, only the long grass was still wet from the heavy rain last night. The views along the coastline stretching from East to West were magnificent, the pinnacles of Beer Head towering above the beach *(see page 174)* and the red cliffs of Sidmouth glowing in the morning sunlight. The countryside has changed since our last walk on 29th Sept, the Blackberries *(see page 176)* are nearly over and the Ash Keys have fallen. I found a few little field Scabious and Hawkbit but along the road through the village the red and white Valerian *(see page 113)* was flowering profusely. The Elderberries are still heavy with fruit but not for long as they are a great favourite of the birds. The trails of Bryony berries were every shade from pale yellow to rich red and I picked some Sloes with a lovely bluish bloom on them. It was mid-afternoon when we left for home and long wispy Mare's Tails were spread across the blue sky in the fading light.

20th Oct. A brilliant red sunrise turning the cliffs pink and tinting all the clouds. The weather is changing, it feels much colder and after the fog and lovely sunshine the storms are blowing up again. The sea is rough and wild with white horses and great long waves are pounding the beach.

22nd Oct. Rolling surf sweeping in and the wind freshening to gale force as overcast skies and sudden rain squalls increased towards the evening. How pleasant it is to sit by the fire as the stormy weather rages outside.

23rd Oct. By this morning the storm had abated but it has been a most wretched day. Heavy rain being blown about by the cold wind made it depressingly miserable just to put one's nose out of doors.

24th Oct. A very still foggy morning. As we drove by the harbour at about 9.15 a.m. the sun was just beginning to break through. High above we could just see a pale blue sky and the faint outlines of fluffy clouds. The tide was very high and the water motionless the pearly-grey shapes of the boats barely visible against the mist enshrouded cliffs *(see page 162)*. There was a quiet stillness as the silvery light of the early morning sun filtered through. For a moment it was a tranquil scene of great beauty but within seconds this dream-world was transformed to reality

Exmoor *(see 16th Oct.)*

173

Beer Head from Branscombe Cliffs *(see 18th Oct.)*

as the fog cleared and the dazzling light reflected from the water brought everything to life. I went to Shapwick to paint the viaduct *(see page 164)*. The sun was quite hot in the sheltered valley and as I worked I could hear the Cows cropping the grass and squelching about in the mud in a field nearby. Eventually they were overcome with curiosity and lined up against the fence to watch me with their big brown, inquisitive eyes, unfortunately bringing swarms of flies with them. At one end of the viaduct the whole bank was covered with Bracken which glowed a rich russet colour in the sunlight and all the hedges and grass were wet with dew. The clouds became sombre and threatening and there were a few drops of rain so I had to cover my work. The sun went in and as the day progressed the wind freshened to gale force with lashing rain and raging seas.

SNUG AND WARM WHILE GALES RAGED

25th Oct. I put down dust sheets and cloths along the window ledges last night and then went to bed and buried myself beneath the bed-clothes, snug and warm whilst the rain pelted down and the gales hissed through the rattling windows. I slept so soundly, the next thing I knew, it was morning. The storm had passed, but during the night it had caused some boats to sink in the river and others to break or drag their moorings. Dark overcast skies soon cleared and the sun came out for a few hours. This evening the sky was a brilliant gold over White Cliff with masses of cream and grey clouds above the sea and silver light shining on the water. Later the dark night sky was divided by a thin horizontal band of pale lemon and turquoise evening light.

26th Oct. Another very foggy morning. It cleared slowly and it was 10.30 a.m. before I could see through the mist the myriad of tiny woolly clouds in the blue sky above. A fiery pink sunset with all the deep-grey clouds suffused with colour.

27th Oct. The morning was damp and chilly and very foggy again. It barely cleared all day but at one time pale shafts of light filtered down through the misty grey clouds illuminating two narrow strips of water on the horizon, one pale silvery orange and the other golden against the calm grey sea. The tide was out and the waves turned lazily on the level stretch of sand exposed by the recent storms. Thick fog again this evening.

29th Oct. I woke early this morning and as I lay in bed listening to the gentle sounds of the sea I could hear the birds singing their dawn chorus. Nothing unusual if you live in the country, but here by the sea with the buildings of the town around us we hear few song birds. The sky was the pale yellow and turquoise of a cold Winter's morning, slowly changing to a warm peachy grey as the sun rose. The hazy golden sphere came from behind the clouds and cast its pale golden light right across the sea from the horizon to the shore then slowly disappeared from view again. Later it reappeared to give us a warm sunny morning but by 2 p.m. it had clouded over and threatened rain.

30th Oct. A deep green choppy sea but no white horses. Heavy rain set in and the wind freshened to gale force, whipping the sea into an angry frenzy.

BLACKBERRY CASTLE

31st Oct. Such a changeable day with brilliant sunshine and heavy rain storms in the morning, then a clear blue sky for a while before a dark mass of ominous cloud appeared. Somewhere the sun broke through, the steely-grey sea banded with gleaming silver light shining down from the heavy rain cloud. We went to Blackberry Castle, the prehistoric earth works. It is a beautiful place with a high bank and dyke surrounding an enclosure covered with short bright green grass dotted with trees. The Autumn sunshine filtered down through the leaves, the glowing colours of the changing foliage gold and russet, amber and green, bright against the long shadows. We saw a Sparrow Hawk perched on a telegraph pole and found the scarlet and orange berries of Bryony and Gladdon *(see pages 90/181)* in the hedgerow. The hedges along the road had been trimmed mechanically, cutting them straight across the top. If only a young sapling could be left to grow here and there to give future generations the beautiful trees our forefathers left for us when they layered the hedges by hand. The moon was already high in the sky as we drove home and the countryside was bathed in the soft warm light of the setting sun. The misty outlines of Winter trees merged into the deep inky-grey of the evening sky and the dark browns of ploughed fields.

Hips *(see 13th Oct.)* **Blackberries** *(see 9th/18th Oct.)*

November

Fog and mist and damp still mornings,
Ghostly shapes of distant trees,
Sudden frosts bring Winter's 'warning',
Fluttering down the last few leaves.

Margaret I. Pogson

Blackberry Castle *(see 1st Nov.)*

178

NOVEMBER

CANNINGTON VIADUCT

1st Nov. It was mild but not very sunny this morning when I returned to Cannington Viaduct to finish my painting *(see pages 164/165)*.
We had to stop at Charton Cross for cattle crossing the road. Two lovely little calves and a brown and white bullock were investigating everything but soon hurried to join the others when they found they were being left behind. Whilst painting, the peace of the countryside was disturbed by a commotion on the hillside. A Crow appeared to be attacking a Jay, chasing it around in circles until it eventually flew off with the crow in hot pursuit. On the way home we saw a Green Woodpecker at Shapwick but it flew away before we were very close *(see page 190)*. In the afternoon we went to Blackberry Castle again and the sun came out for a short while, lighting up all the lovely Autumn colours of the trees *(see page 178)*. I would like to return in the Spring when all the leaves are fresh and green and the Blue Bells are out. The sky became overcast and it rained heavily, turning much colder towards the evening. Just before going to bed, I went on the roof to read the thermometer and found the moon shining brightly from a clear sky – often a sign of frost.

Old Man's Beard
(see 18th/25th Nov.)

2nd Nov. The temperature fell to just about freezing point last night and the dawn was clear and bright with a very light mist over the surface of the sea. It remained sunny all day, turning much milder towards the evening but the wind freshened and the sea became quite rough, promising a stormy night.

4th Nov. There wasn't a soul in sight when I walked along the seafront this morning and it was so quiet and peaceful with just the sound of the sea and the cry of Gulls. The whole scene was subdued, low grey clouds over the cliffs, a silver grey sky on the horizon above the choppy grey-green sea.

6th Nov. The S.W. wind turned to gale force in the night and I woke to the rattling of doors and windows and the whistling of the wind through any odd gap it could find. The day was mild but very cloudy and by evening it was raining again.

7th Nov. A very dull, overcast morning with occasional light drizzle yet despite the weather we set out to walk to Colyton by Waterside, Axmouth, the footpath to Axbridge and the river Coly. It was very tranquil by the river so we sat on the stile just before Coles Mill and had some hot coffee from a flask. The current was strong, with swirling eddies in the deep water and along the banks a few flowers of Indian Balsam had survived the frosts. The rain began to set in so we crossed the footbridge to the road and tuned for home. Tucked away in the hedgerows I noticed the Dogwood *(see page 143)* flowering again and a few bright Campion and Toadflax. Some Ivy had both flowers and berries on the same stem and earlier when we were walking along the Waterside I found some bushes covered in Hops. The rain was torrential and we were very fortunate to get a lift back to Seaton as ominous dark clouds gathered in the evening sky over White Cliff. I was pleased to get home, to change out of my wet clothes and dry my hair and sit by the warm fire.

9th Nov. The cloud formations are glorious at this time of year and were particularly beautiful this afternoon. All along the Southern horizon, over the sea, there were pyramid shaped clouds in rich greys and creams with blue sky above and a pinky-grey haze below.

Earth Star *(see 15th Nov.)*

10th Nov. The weather continues to be quiet and still, gradually turning colder with a frost this morning. There was a dazzling golden sunrise with great shafts of light shining down accentuating the dark mass of rain clouds in the West and heavy showers continued throughout the day. During the afternoon the low cloud blotted out the light yet towards Shute the distant hills were in brilliant sunshine which made them appear much nearer. Shute House, all the fields and the Autumn colours of the trees in the woods, were quite distinct. As evening fell, dense misty grey clouds touched with red and fiery-pink swirled across the sky. They billowed out over the sea to a mass of dark grey and brilliant pink fading into the horizon.

11th Nov. It suddenly turned very stormy this afternoon, the sky heavy with great grey clouds. The wind blustered and blew the lashing rain and the sea became wild but by late evening there were signs of it abating.

12th Nov. The storm must have blown itself out during the night as the morning dawned bright and still. The clouds were beautiful this afternoon, warm grey against the pink sky and forever changing, with great shafts of light down to the sea.

Gladdon
(see 31st Oct. and 21st Nov.)

Puffball

Pinhay Beach *(see 15th Nov.)*

13th Nov. The first real wintry day with frosted ferns patterned on all the windows when we got up this morning. Everything was white with frost at Seaton but at Rousdon and Uplyme most of it had thawed by mid-morning when we left for Taunton. The countryside lay silent and still beneath the cold misty air and low grey cloud. The Autumn colours of the trees and fresh green tangles of Mistletoe were crisp with frost. It began to rain and by mid-afternoon was stormy and wild with blustery winds swirling the leaves from the trees and tumbling them along the road to gather in the gutters. The storm heightened, raging and howling around the flat all night.

14th Nov. The storm abated during the night and there was brilliant sunshine for most of the day but a very heavy hail storm around noon. There was a wintry chill in the air as I walked along the Old Beer Road, and the damp smell of rotting leaves. The sky was a drifting jumble of clouds, all cream and grey. As evening closed in, they became sombre and dark against the cold yellow light of the setting sun.

15th Nov. Although the sky was heavy with low grey cloud and it was spotting with rain, I decided to go ahead with the cliff walk I had planned from Whitlands to Pinhay Beach. We had been told it may be overgrown so were not surprised to find a rough track and spent some time scrambling over banks and through the undergrowth before we realised we had taken a wrong turning. It began to pour with rain and looked as though it was settling in for the day so we made our way back to the road. Only a few yards further on we found the grassy opening of the right path concealed by the bushes and as the rain was easing off and the sky looked brighter we decided to carry on. Two trees had fallen across the narrow track but we managed to squeeze under one and clamber over the other and continue on our way. There were still some Autumn fruits about; Sweet Chestnuts, Hazel Nuts and the berries of Privet and St John's Wort and various fungi growing under the trees. One kind I had not seen before, the pale ivory and pink Earth Stars which rest on the surface of the ground and can be picked up like fallen Apples as they have no roots or are attached in any way *(see page 180)*. We startled a Pheasant and it flew up noisily from the undergrowth.

The Cliffs, Beer *(see 20th Nov.)*

Mill on the Coly *(see 21st Nov.)*

Just as we reached the field gate to the Landslip path, the sun broke through the clouds lighting up all the colours of the Beech Trees and the rich russet carpet of leaves on the track before us. We came to the pumping station in the clearing and then it was just a short way down the rough steps to the beach.

SHELLS AND FOSSILS ON PINHAY BEACH *(see page 182/183)*

We had our sandwiches and coffee, sitting on the rocks in the sunshine, watching the tide come in. How I love that stretch of beach, the peace and solitude and always so many interesting things to see. I spent some time searching the small pebbles and grit between the larger stones and became so engrossed, I often received a cold shower as the incoming tide crept up on me and broke against the rocks nearby. There were numerous tiny shells of pale delicate pink, yellow and striped and some small fossils but my greatest find was where the cliff had recently fallen. There in the Blue Lias was exposed a perfect specimen of Ammonite about 18 ins across. It was much too heavy to move or I would have tried to carry it home or put it somewhere safe from the sea. There was a cold wind and we began to feel chilly so we packed up our things and returned the way we had come, stopping at Rousdon to pick sacks full of Bracken for the garden.

18th Nov. Heavy rain and hail storms with intermittent sun-shine. In the afternoon I went down the Marsh Path to pick some Old Man's Beard and found it trailing over the trees and shrubs in pearly-grey cascades of fluff *(see page 179)*. There were some Lords and Ladies seed heads tucked away in the shelter of the hedge but the Bryony berries had been spoiled by the hard frosts *(see page 191)*. The trees were nearly bare and everywhere was very wet and muddy with rotting leaves underfoot.

Sunset over the Axe Estuary *(see 29th Nov.)*

189

20th Nov. A very foggy morning and although the sun broke through and it appeared to be clearing it soon closed in again. From the top of Seaton Down Hill it was impossible to see the valley. In the afternoon I went to the Coly between Colyton and Colyford, crossing the little footbridge over the river and walking along the bank past the weir. I disturbed a Heron fishing at the water's edge and it took off, spreading its large wings and flying low over the water. It slowly gained height and turning, made off over trees. I sat for about an hour listening to the water rippling over the stones as I painted and would have enjoyed the quiet stillness even longer had it not been so cold and damp as the fog settled. On returning home I looked out at the wintry grey of sky and sea and noticed a beautiful effect of light around Beer Head *(see pages 184/185)*. It was silhouetted, dark grey, against a pale pink halo of light and just beneath the headland at water level there sparkled a thin line of glittering pink sea.

GREEN WOODPECKER

21st Nov. This morning I watched a Green Woodpecker on the lawn in Kathleen's garden *(see page 179 and below)*. We could see it clearly as it pecked at something in the turf, the brilliant red head, greenback, yellowish rump and black and white bars on its wings. It flew off and settled vertically on a tree. I went to

Green Woodpecker
(see 1st/21st Nov.)

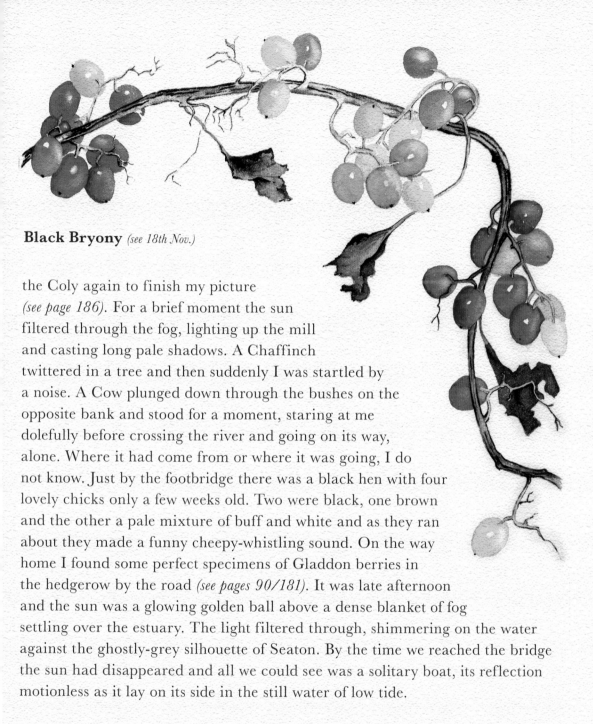

Black Bryony *(see 18th Nov.)*

the Coly again to finish my picture
(see page 186). For a brief moment the sun
filtered through the fog, lighting up the mill
and casting long pale shadows. A Chaffinch
twittered in a tree and then suddenly I was startled by
a noise. A Cow plunged down through the bushes on the
opposite bank and stood for a moment, staring at me
dolefully before crossing the river and going on its way,
alone. Where it had come from or where it was going, I do
not know. Just by the footbridge there was a black hen with four
lovely chicks only a few weeks old. Two were black, one brown
and the other a pale mixture of buff and white and as they ran
about they made a funny cheepy-whistling sound. On the way
home I found some perfect specimens of Gladdon berries in
the hedgerow by the road *(see pages 90/181)*. It was late afternoon
and the sun was a glowing golden ball above a dense blanket of fog
settling over the estuary. The light filtered through, shimmering on the water
against the ghostly-grey silhouette of Seaton. By the time we reached the bridge
the sun had disappeared and all we could see was a solitary boat, its reflection
motionless as it lay on its side in the still water of low tide.

24th Nov. A bright clear morning white with frost and a light mist over the surface
of the sea. The water was so still, only gently lapping the patches of sand exposed
by the low tide. There was brilliant sunshine and blue sky all day, fading at eventide
to pale yellow and green with dark clouds gathering over Beer Head against pale
orange light. A thin crescent of moon came up like a childhood drawing of the
Man-in-the-Moon and the night was crisp and clear.

A TIDING OF MAGPIES

25th Nov. We saw a Tiding of Magpies today on Atkins Hill, near Uplyme.
There were at least five and possibly as many as seven congregating in some bushes.
They looked quite startling in their brilliant blue-black and white plumage. The trees
in the hollow were draped from top to bottom with cascades of pearly-grey Old Man's
Beard which looked lovely against the yellowy brown of the Autumn foliage *(see page
179).* Some trees are already quite bare whilst others hardly appear to have lost a leaf.
A very mild day but with strong S.W. winds off the sea topping the choppy cold
green waves with white horses.

26th Nov. Very mild to the point of being warm but overcast and dull. White water
churned onto the beach all day with a light mist part drizzle, part spray drifting
across the seafront.

28th Nov. The sun rose, a glowing fiery ball on the edge of a dark cloud over
the sea but gradually turning golden became a beautiful sunny day.

29th Nov. I went to the top of Seaton Down Hill this afternoon to paint the
landscape but the subdued light and mist over the valley made it difficult to
distinguish the distant hills of Axmouth or the sea from the sky. Occasionally the
pale sunlight touched a group of trees or a field, bringing a flicker of colour to the
countryside and turning the river Axe into a silver ribbon *(see pages 188/189).*
We returned home by Axmouth, stopping at the roadside just before the village
to watch the fading light of evening. Seaton and Beer Head were misty silhouettes
against the pale grey and apricot sunset with the blue sky above a drift with cream
Mare's Tails. The pale water of the river shimmered with blinding golden light where
the last of the sun's rays lay across its path. The dark speckles of a flock of birds
skimmed the surface and in the cold stillness we could
hear the cries of Curlews.

**Shells &
Fossils**
(see 15th Nov.)

December

Golden sunlight palely gleaming,
Vivid sunsets paint the sky,
Mother Nature soundly sleeping,
To stir anew when Spring is nigh.

Margaret I. Pogson

Frosty Morning, Axmouth

DECEMBER

1st Dec. Very mild and damp with occasional light drizzle.

3rd Dec. It has been a lovely mild day with bright sunshine. Towards evening it turned colder with a full moon high in a clear sky twinkling with stars but there were no reflections across the sea. I could hear the cry of a Curlew above the sound of the waves.

SILVER SEA

4th Dec. Today we walked over the cliffs to Beer, stopping to look back at the crests of white water sweeping in across the bay. Some of the cliff has fallen again and a new fence has had to be erected by the path. After buying fresh fish from the little shop on the beach, we sat for a while watching the Gulls feed on the large areas of seaweed exposed by the low Spring tide. Others wheeled and glided on the wind, their strident cries resounding from the cliffs. We climbed over the rocks at the end of the breakwater and returned along the beach, picking our way between the pools and taking care not to slip on the seaweed. The rocks were encrusted with limpets and winkles *(see page 196)* and we found some coloured stones, beautifully marked. At Seaton Hole there was a large area of smooth glistening wet sand, gentle ripples curving across its surface after each small wave. The sun broke through the clouds, lighting up the distant cliffs and streaming down in shafts of light to turn the sea to silver on the horizon. We watched a bird of prey hovering on the blustery wind until it dropped like a stone on its unfortunate victim.

6th Dec. It was dark when I left for Lincolnshire this morning. A shadowy moon appeared briefly between the stormy clouds and the high water in the Axe was still and grey. As I travelled to London the dawn broke through the heavy cloud, glowing pink in the pale light of the sky. I find little pleasure in the Lincolnshire Fenlands, especially at this time of the year when they are so bleak and inhospitable. The old farmsteads and trees silhouetted against the wide skies can be very picturesque but so much has been destroyed by modern farming methods. How I loathe those vast fields devoid of trees or hedges, the monotony, the lack of shelter for wildlife. I remember only too well, the dust storms in Summer and the stench of chemical sprays. But I love the old windmills, the Maud Foster at Boston and the eight-sailed giant at Heckington which I always look for as I pass on the train.

10th Dec. There was torrential rain yesterday evening which returned again after bright sunshine for most of today.

11th Dec. It was very wet when I left Lincolnshire this morning. On the journey home I saw flooded fields and swollen rivers, swirling with muddy water. At Seaton I found they had had terrific storms and howling gales on the 9th and 10th which had fortunately abated at about 6 p.m. yesterday, averting the possibility of severe flooding.

Winkle Limpets   **Common Starfish**   **Snakelocks Anemone**   **Shrimp**
(see 4th Dec.)   *(see 9th Oct.)*   *(see 9th Oct.)*

12th Dec. It has been very wild all day with the roar of the sea, howling winds and lashing rain.

PERFECT WINTER'S MORNING

13th Dec. A perfect Winter's morning, so clear, with pale sunlight breaking through and cold breeze off the sea. In the afternoon I went to the top of Seaton Down Hill to paint the view looking across the valley *(see pages 200/201)*. The clouds were beautiful above the misty hues of the bare trees and wintry countryside. The river Axe lay in the valley, silver and grey with Axmouth nestling between the hills and the sea pale in the afternoon sunlight. The days are so short now that by 3 p.m. the light was already fading and outlines becoming so indistinct I could not work any longer. It began to spot with rain and by evening was bucketing down.

orpion Fish   **Beadlet Anemone**   **Hermit Crab**   **Snakelocks Anemone**
(see 9th Oct.)   *(see 9th Oct.)*   *(see 9th Oct.)*

Axmouth Pottery *(see 14th Dec.)*

View from Seaton Down Hill *(see 13th Dec.)*

14th Dec. A bright clear morning with the sunshine quite warm but a cold wind. I walked to Axmouth along Waterside, the tide was high and there were many waterfowl on the river but they were too far away to identify. Two Mallard Ducks and three beautiful Drakes were swimming together at the water's edge. There were still a few dark red Haws and some scarlet Hips in the hedgerows and the brilliant orange seed heads of Gladdon amongst the grass. The pale lavender flowers of Lesser Periwinkle were spread out on the bank under the hedges, no doubt bought on by the mild weather as they are usually not in bloom until January or February. The Winter Heliotrope *(see page 202)* was also in full flower along the roadside. I went to the pottery to paint but my heart sank when I saw row upon row of pots on racks, they were all shapes and sizes and every shade of raw Umber to Off-white, becoming paler as they dried out *(see page 198/199)*. Eventually they would be fired, glazed

and re-fired to produce the potters own distinctive type of ware. It was late afternoon when I left, the sun had set and the wind was cold by the river. It was dark and lonely and it began to rain so I hurried home to the warmth and comfort of the fireside. During the evening a gale blew up, the wind blustering and howling as the rain pelted down.

VIOLENT STORM

15th Dec. At about 1.45 a.m. a violent storm awoke us with bright flashes of lightning over the sea and the wind howling and shrieking for nearly two hours. Great masses of white water broke on the shore, sweeping up the beach and flooding the road further along the Esplanade. In the morning it was still wild, the wind blowing mists of spray from the white crests of the waves as they rolled in 10-15 feet high to crash thunderously in great cascades of water. At low tide the beach was quite flat with large areas of smooth sand and fine shingle, it was a day of sudden squalls sweeping across the valley with sunny spells, as the massive clouds drifted apart to reveal patches of blue sky. A complete rainbow spread itself across the sky, one end in the town and the other out at sea. As I walked to Beer in the afternoon great rays of golden light fell upon the sea and as each wave receded the pebbles shone like silver. Two Pied Wagtails scurried about the West Walk and a perky little Robin sitting on a twig by the cliff path looked at me as if to ask for food. As evening closed in the wind freshened and there was heavy rain but it abated before bedtime.

17th Dec. At last there are definite signs of the building of the new sea wall. Some weeks ago surveyors were busy with their red and white poles but today a large crane has arrived and is unloading steel piles all along the sea-front. There has been much controversy over the plans and although the final design is more attractive as it includes a promenade, I fear splitting of the original wave-return will make it less effective.

18th Dec. It has turned much colder and is still very wet with sudden heavy rain squalls during the morning. In the afternoon the clouds cleared and the sun came out for a while as I walked to Axmouth to paint again at the pottery, it was low tide and the birds were feeding on the mud-flats which were still so wet they reflected all the colours of the sky, pink and blue, green and grey. When I returned home at about 4.15 p.m. it was dusk and the tide was high, the wide stretch of water pale against the deepening shadows of evening.

19th Dec. When I woke this morning the bedroom wall was pink from the fiery glow of the sunrise. I looked out on to a cold clear morning but as the day brightened golden sunlight shone from a blue sky but the wind remained bitterly cold. I returned, yet again, to the top of Seaton Down Hill this afternoon when the view was perfect in the clear wintry light. I could see the bridge over the

Winter Heliotrope *(see 14th Dec.)*

Axe, Seaton Church and the Old Vicarage at Axmouth and all the fields such
a brilliant green as the grass has continued to grow during the mild weather. As the
sunset and the shadows lengthened, the countryside took on a golden hue gradually
turning to rose. The evening sky was a clear blue and green with mauve-grey clouds
tinted with yellowy-pink, all slowly changing to deep dusky crimson. I think there will
be a frost tonight as it is turning even colder as the wind freshens from the North.

RED SUNRISE AND GOLDEN SUNSET

20th Dec. Another brilliant red sunrise over a pale turquoise sea and sunshine for
most of the day. I went to the Coly Fields to paint Hamlyn's Mill *(see page 204)* and found
much of the foliage by the bridge had been cleared away and a wall built down into the
river. The hedge has gone and a wooden fence erected and although it looks very neat
and tidy, another home for the birds has been destroyed and countryside loses a little
more of its charm. Two Moorhens dabbled in the river as I painted but I didn't share
their company for long as half an hour is about as much as one can manage to sit outside
at this time of year, before fingers and toes become numb with cold. We came home
through Axmouth, stopping at the roadside just before the village to watch the sun set
over the river. It was beyond description, a great sweep of brilliant changing light, rich
mauve and deep pink with the sun a glowing golden ball. The Axe was
a sheet of still, pink water contrasting with the mud flats alive with
thousands of birds feeding as the light slowly faded.

21st Dec. A sharp frost last night with only a glimpse
of pale wintry sunlight today. The sky had the dense
grey look of threatening snow and sure enough
by early evening some had fallen on the
high ground between the water-tower and
Honiton. During the afternoon the clouds
parted over Beer Head revealing
a brilliant copper-coloured sky with
a single ray of light falling to the
sea and shimmering in a narrow
path across the water.

Pine

Hamlyn's Mill *(see 20th Dec.)*

23rd Dec. The day has been quiet and still without a breath of wind. At Axmouth the smoke from a bonfire and some chimneys drifted lazily upwards, not a curl nor a curve disturbing its heavenward course. Despite the mildness of the morning there remained some frost and snow at Rousdon. The tide was very high in the river and the wide stretch of water so motionless each tiny detail had a perfect reflection, even to all the colour and movement to a flock of seabirds flying overhead. And yet, when we returned about two hours later the tide was ebbing so rapidly each buoy made a wide rippling 'V' in the water as the current flowed swiftly past. Late in the afternoon I walked along the beach to Seaton Hole and found it almost deserted and with such a magical atmosphere, as though it was isolated from the rest of the world. I stood for a while at the water's edge with just the sound of the waves and the distant cry of a Gull. A number of small birds busied themselves at the foot of the cliff, a Chaffinch, a Wagtail, the quick glimpse of the scarlet breast of a Robin and two perky little Wrens. As I made my way home I could feel the chill of evening settling in.

24th Dec. A really beautiful day of brilliant sunshine from a blue sky from sunrise until the golden sunset but with a nip in the air.

BITTERLY COLD

25th Dec. It was bitterly cold last night and white all over with frost this morning with the temperature only 18° F. The windows were patterned with ferns and icicles hung from the sill. At Beer Head a thin veil of mist drifted at sea level the effect eerie and mystical in the early morning light. The sun shone brilliantly for most of the day but it was late afternoon before I went to the boat-yard to see how Brian had progressed with his boat. It was still so cold the rainwater that had collected in some small craft was frozen solid. We walked home along the beach as the recent storms had flattened the high shingle banks leaving a gently sloping shore of firm sand and small pebbles swept clean with a rush of white-edged water as each wave broke. Two Seagulls wheeled and glided stark white against the threatening storm clouds gathering in the sky and dark rays of heavy rain falling to the sea. To the East the sky was a sombre blue and the sea blue and grey but in the West the waves were emerald green becoming black on the horizon. As the storm swept across Beer Head to White Cliff, the mists of falling rain became suffused with light against paler grey clouds and a clear yellow sky above. We hurried home but before we could reach shelter it was upon us. It turned much milder in the evening but the wind freshened from the S.W. bringing heavy seas.

26th Dec. There were reports of an earthquake in Scotland and Northern England early this morning. It read nearly 5 on the Richter Scale and lasted about 10 seconds but no severe damage was done. It was an odd coincidence that sometime after 12.30 p.m. last night I felt a very slight tremble of the bed and put it down to the ferocity of storm raging outside.

LASHING RAIN AND ROARING SEAS

27th Dec. The storm continued, howling and screaming all last night with lashing rain and roaring seas. At noon it was over the low sea wall but there was no real need for alarm and by 8 p.m. all had gone quiet except for the beating rain. This morning the jetty in the harbour was completely covered at high tide with only the railings showing and at Axmouth waves were breaking over the picnic area. The fence by the river was under water and there was a small stream running down Boshill, swirling across the road as it cascaded over debris. The Axe Valley is like a huge lake with little islands of trees and still it rains!

28th Dec. As the water drains from the surrounding hills, the floods continue to rise and have now reached Seaton. This morning there was a Heron fishing in the fore-court of the Blue Waters Holiday Camp.

29th Dec. The morning dawned quiet and still with a calm sea gently breaking on the shore. Misty, light cloud began to form in the sky over Shute gradually becoming a dark violet-grey and sweeping down the valley bringing rain and hail which settled in sheltered corners. I went to collect some Mistletoe *(see page 207)* from an old apple tree stump in Harepath Road, then continued on through Colyford. The floods have washed away part of the old stone wall leading to the bridge over the Axe.

30th Dec. I walked along the beach to the mouth of the Axe this
afternoon to see the effects of the floods. The sheer volume of water leaving
the river has taken away considerable amounts of the shingle bank, making
the mouth much wider. The sunlight was golden, bringing a warm glow
to Haven Cliff and the old bridge and picking out the colours of the boats
moored at the quay. There were two Cormorants diving in the river, one
of them looking very waterlogged. It was making for the shore, probably
to dry its feathers but swam away when it saw me, slowly sinking until only
its head and neck were visible. I was so afraid it would drown. The flood
water has completely disappeared from the marshes.

Holly and Mistletoe *(see 29th Dec.)*

FULL-CIRCLE

31st Dec. The last day of the year. There was a
brilliant sunrise of red and golden light against a cold
wintry sky. It was a beautiful still Winter's day, a pale
blue-grey sky blending into a calm blue-grey sea with
only the gentle murmur of ripples on the shore.
A few distant clouds were suspended on the horizon
and the pale, hazy sunlight sparkled on the water.
As the sun reached its full height a brilliant gleam
of light spread across the sea to the shore. Just before
I went to bed I looked out of the window. Around the
moon there was a wide halo and from the clear sky
the silvery light shone brightly over sea and cliffs.
For a moment I stood, enchanted, then feeling the cold
I turned away, closed the curtains and crept into bed.
And so the seasons have turned full-circle
and another year has slipped away.

Margaret J. Pogson.